CW01403485

BE

THYSELF

THE PATH OF FREEDOM, FULFILMENT AND ABUNDANCE

MUZIRE MBUENDE

Copyright © 2019 by Muzire Mbuende.

All rights reserved. No part of this book may be
reproduced or transmitted in any form or by any means,
electronic or mechanical, including photocopying,
recording, or by any information storage and retrieval
system, without permission in writing from the copyright
owner.

ACKNOWLEDGEMENTS

It is because of the gift of life in human form that, I am able to pen this material. My immense gratitude goes to Him who grants life. •

This book holds tribute to my grandmother, Justine Kangootui- a woman of soft wisdom and extraordinary love. She did a phenomenal job in making sure I integrated well into this world of matter, playing her role with a gentle voice and careful words. It is my firm conviction that, "Justy" comes from the crop of the souls that were cut from the colourful and rich cloth of love, generosity and kindness. Those caring and steadfast human beings who for some reason never uttered the words, 'I love you', but those close to them and, those who came in contact with them was never left in ambiguity of the kind of love that emanated from their souls. Like all of them, her love was hidden in her vibe; in the way she would engage you, you could feel it just in the way she would hold and rub your hands, I felt it just in the way she would apply wine and oil on my wounds when I was but a boy. In her highest deeds and grandest expression - her love was so radiant and intense that even in the absence of expressing it in words - its authenticity and warmth was made known. Rest easy "Justy".

My gratitude also extends to Noah Mbuende, who in silence has shaped my conduct, and to Thabita Mbuende and Dr. Evelyn U. Kaambo. Two gracious women of extraordinary love. The former, a selfless woman who has a taken a role in my life never ordained to her by nature but, dared to occupy that space and made it her own – with grace and elegance. In her care I have become the man I am – Such commendable personalities hold inspiration.

Finally, I would like to show my appreciation to every soul that has impacted my life in one way or the other. I withhold your names for your privacy and to preserve the space you currently occupy. Although you are anonymous, thank you for shaping me, in your own unique way.

This book is dedicated to you.

vi

TABLE OF CONTENTS

PREFACE

We must work for the bread and fish we put on the table, for the oil and wine that would heal our wounds, for only from the sweat of our brow shall we produce food to eat and have a dime to afford the accessories of life; this is an undeniable fact. Unfortunately, it appears that in our society we have become so absorbed in making a living that we have no time left for living itself. A man should not work to live but, should live inspired to work. Nevertheless, we continue with this conventional life draining paradigm and along the journey we find ourselves with ever a feeling of discontentment and longing for more within our hearts, which we think we will fill and satisfy by buying the most beautiful accessories, or by hanging out at the coolest entertainment joints in town. We try to subdue this longing through constant round of pleasure and entertainment, but its hunger is immense. Our souls continue to feel dissatisfied and empty. We can quench the thirst of our flesh with earthy water and can rid of hunger by filling our bellies with earthly food, but there is something within us that will never be satisfied with any one accessory or food that we can find on the face of the earth.

There is a thing within us, a product, a light, something that longs to be brought out, and it is the silencing and suppression of this thing with other line of work that is not in alignment with who we really are that, we have given birth to a feeling of longing and discontentment within our hearts. This thing needs nothing from the external to satisfy its hunger, all it ever yearns for is the highest expression of itself and in this sleeps our own liberty and joy and so the advancement and betterment of life.

I do not intent to erect a new wall of truth, before which men would come and bow down in search for grace and invocation. My motive with this material is simply to remind every man who reads and embraces the principles conveyed in it, of himself. To tell him, if he will believe, what his real nature is, to inform him there is engraved in his soul a unique and perfect self-expression, to tell him as an individual to be original and encourage him to do the most distinctive thing possible to him, to tell him to get on the path of his true design, to instruct him to surrender to the calling on his life, to that sacred something - his god-element, for in that courageous and selfless act is his great opportunity for a fuller, expanded self-expression; a great chance for him to march forward, onward and Godward to a place where liberty and joy dwells.

You will notice that the same principles and concepts has been repeated throughout this book, and deliberately so, because we want to make sure we drive some ideas home.

Please note that references to "man" and "men" must be read as referring to both male and female, interpreted as humanity.

INTRODUCTION

Something has called you into being for a unique thing you are to express in this world. There is call on your life for a service you are to render – your life's work. Florence Scovel Shinn knew this to be true when she said, "There is for each man, perfect self-expression. There is a place which he is to fill and no one else can fill, something he is to do, which no one else can do: it is his destiny!" There is indeed a space that you are to occupy that no one else can occupy – a role you are to play, a solution you are to bring, a baton you are to light that was solely designated unto you by the Power from which you have come from.

Also united in this eternal truth was Marten Oiresin for he said, "If nature has called you to a position, if the call runs in your blood, it is a part of your life and you cannot get away from it. It is not a separate thing from yourself. It exists in every brain cell, every nerve cell; every blood corpuscle contains some of it. You can no more get away from it than a leopard can get away from his spots...' '... for the thing he was made for is as much a part of his real being as his temperament. It is nearer to him than his heart-beat, closer than his breath. There is a photograph of the thing he was made for, in every cell in his body. He cannot get away from it. The thing which will make the life distinctive, which will make it a power, is the one supreme thing which we want to do, and feel that we must do; and, no matter how long we may be delayed from this aim, or how far we may be swerved aside by mistakes or iron circumstances, we should never give up hope or a determination to pursue our object. Some people have not the moral courage, the persistence, the force of character, to get the things out of the way which stand between them and their ambition. They allow themselves to be pushed this way and that way into things for which they have no fitness or taste. Their will power is not strong enough to enable them to fight their way to their goal. They are pushed aside by the pressure about them and do the things for which they have little or no liking or adaptation. If there is anything in the world a person should fight for, it is freedom to pursue his ideal" ... "If he does not pursue his ideal, does not carry out his supreme aim, his life will be more or less of a failure, no matter how much he may be actuated by a sense of duty, or how much he may exert his will."

The beauty of a flower sleeps within and so does your own unique self-expression. There is a vision of this (unique self-expression) that has been planted inside your soul. There is a picture of this in the superconscious mind. It usually flashes across the conscious mind as you go about your life affairs. A calling, a gentle whisper inside of you telling you that this is the work you are to carry out.

You already know this truth, and by reading this – this truth resonates – there is a sudden but a gentle confirmation and a remembrance of this truth within you right now. And with this material, I am here to solely remind and awaken you to the truth you already know. For it is our truth, our knowing – eternally engraved within our souls.

Imagine a life where you wake up feeling fulfilled, happy, and ready to do only the thing you want to. This is the promise that is embedded in your calling – your life's work. But you can only taste this promise, when you courageously decide to follow and live out the vision that has been planted in you. Any other form of being that is not in alignment with Who You Really Are – is a meaningless way of being and a life spent in vain, and through your own feelings, by not feeling so good about your life, this truth will be whispered to you. Your duty is to listen and honor this whisper.

This is the path taken by the most creative people the world has ever known, the ones who led revolutions of their kind and who discovered and invented extraordinary things. This is the path that was designated to every human soul, if he but dares to shut out the external cacophony and listen to his silent inner-voice. If he learns and honors this voice and allows it to fully and unashamedly express itself, he will be able to express that which moves and dances his soul, a path that will forevermore quench and satisfy the thirst and hunger of his soul.

Isn't it interesting that we all want the same things in life? Financial freedom, abundance, peace, happiness, joy, and the freedom to do what we want. Yet only a select few manage to enjoy these privileges in life. Are the majority of men deliberately fishing in shallow waters? Or is there a fundamental law and principle that only a select few understand and employ? Is there something the majority of men do not seem to understand, of the way of life, the understanding of which will change everything? Indeed, there is. The few men who have creatively arrived successfully in life know how to cast their nets. I will reveal in this book the proven approach and principle that those successful men are employing, and once you also employ it, you will become, do, and have anything you desire in this world.

I do not intend to write a book of wonder, or a book claiming to prevent an unsavoury future. I intend to provide you the only creative, tested, and proven blueprint that will enable to achieve your dreams. It is the intent of this book to bring you an awareness of your true design, and what you need to do in order to remove the heavy yoke of confusion and fear in you, which is preventing you to express your uniqueness.

As a lifetime student of the laws of the universe, and as a seeker of truth concerning the principles and habits that leads to success and freedom, I have seen this principle acting out in the lives of almost every top achiever, from Oprah Winfrey to Bob Proctor, to Tony Robbins. I have discovered a fundamental life principle that all the top performers, influencers and business people employ to be, do, and have everything they have hoped for. I seek to show a tested and confirmed method of success any person can embrace into their lives.

This principle will only work if you work it. Oprah was fired from her first television job as an anchor in Baltimore, but she listened to the voice in her soul rather than to the pessimistic external opinions and voices and kept with the principle, and her consistency was proven to be sound. Bob Proctor and Les Brown had no college degree, but they employed the principle deliberately and to the letter, and their achievement is testament that the principle works if you work with it.

Limitless prosperity will become real to you, but there is a formula on how to unlock and inherit it. It is a less stressful route to a life of simplistic happiness, untold prosperity and all good things in greater measure. That route is just to *'Be Thyself'*, which in turn will prompt you to *'do'* the thing you are born to do, and the accessories of life will be given unto you a hundredfold.

There is no more joyful being-ness than inspired being-ness, and there is no more exciting doing-ness than inspired action. This is the way to work *with* the Law of Life and the Creative Powers of the universe, and not *against* them.

You know that you were meant for something great, you know that there is more for you. Yet you are selling yourself short by being and doing exactly what everyone else is doing. That might not be who you are. It is no coincidence that you are longing to be more, for the limitless Spirit within you is seeking the highest expression of itself. For what it knows itself to be.

What is to come is both intriguing and informative, based solely on the principle of working with the Law of the universe. Each chapter will give you new insight as you strive to achieve your vision. You are not reading this material by coincidence. You have always sought this truth, and now that you have received it, you must put it to good use.

As a result of inspiration, may every soul that drinketh from this cup not merely and idly sing that great ancient lyric, "This little light of mine, I am gonna let it shine", but develop the necessary mental tenacity coupled with action so that he may courageously toss away the bushel basket that has robbed him of his birthright freedom, fulfillment and abundance, and allow his perfect self-expression to shine in its full glory – sure.

CHAPTER 1
WHO?

Who You Really Are

"At the center of your being you have the answer; you know who you are and you know what you want." — *Lao Tzu*

The question before every man is, '**Who am I?**'

In the beginning, God/Spirit existed in a state of being, without the means to express and experience Himself/Itself. God/Spirit conceptually knew Himself/Itself to be infinite but was without a medium through which infinity could be explored or experienced; thus, infinity remained nothing unto itself. God was miraculous and loving but was without the mode to express his miracles and love. God's soul sought to express and experience itself, but expression is impossible without form. Thus, God created form, (man and all of creation), solely to serve as a means or a vehicle through which His soul can express and experience His qualities that only existed as a concept prior to creation. Every living man and creation at large acts as an individualized branch of the Infinite Father, through which the sap of Life-Spirit seeks to flow to give birth to the dreams and creations of God Himself. As God's dream, you were created out of a fine material, sculpted out of beautiful fabric, and out of divine light you were molded. Infinite-Intelligence assembled you perfectly in the darkness within the belly, all to allow the power from which you have come from to reveal itself through you. God made you out of Himself, because His soul yearns to express and experience Itself through you.

You are merely an agent, and alive not because you give life to yourself; but you are a living creation to serve as a medium through which the Intelligent and Limitless Spirit can feel and see Itself in you, through and as you. The garment of flesh and blood is seemingly alive because of the Spirit which has chosen to express itself through it, and the Spirit as life itself cannot help but give life to the form (which is your body, through which) it seeks to express and experience its qualities. You are Divinity confined by Humanity. Your body is merely an envelope of the Soul. The birds, foxes, and trees are not alive because they give life to themselves; they are powered with life through a Greater Being. Therefore, we find truth in "I am the resurrection and the life…" as well as "I am the way, the truth, and the life" Consciousness and the Spirit is the only truth, the only thing that bears life.

As an electrical wire will not be "live" unless there is an electrical current flowing through it, So would we not be "powered" and be "alive" unless there is a Life-Force seeking to express and experience itself through us. Therefore, our Consciousness is not one with our bodies; our flesh merely conducts the expression (or the spiritual current) of a Substance bigger than ourselves. We are not the device, but rather, we are the very Spirit seeking to reveal itself through us. This I believe, is what Jesus meant when he said, "I and the Father are one." For In a similar manner, as there is only one entity that is the real power in electrical systems: the *'electricity'* itself, there is in us only one entity that is the true power: The Life-Force itself. Jesus termed it as his Father, some call it the Presence, some say it is God, some in various circles recognize it as Consciousness. Whatever name you want to call it. The fact is, it is, it exists. If there is any man on the earth that can make the blind see, it is not his flesh that heals, but the power within him, expressing itself through his flesh. If there is a genius on this earth with a renowned invention, it is all because of the Infinite Intelligence within him seeking to reveal its greatness.

This is the very power seeking to express itself through you, by a means of itself. This is Who You Really Are.

"You are That Which Is;

You are not your name,
You are not your body either; you merely inhabit your body.
Your body is just a means, a garment of skin, flesh and bones,

created from dust, clothed unto you in the belly, as a means for that which is within you to express, explore and experience itself fully. You are a spirit expressing and experiencing itself through a human form." –*Muzire Mbuende (2015)*

We do not think and feel due to our own choosing, but solely because thoughts and feelings are the essence and livingness of the Spirit. We do not imagine because we have developed a faculty of imagination on our own. We imagine because imagination is the very method through which the Father creates, and through which everything in the universe was made that was made, and through which everything is still being made that is being made, and through which everything will still be made that will ever be made. We do not create because it is of our own choosing and longing; we create because creating, expressing, expanding, and experiencing is the desire of the Father. Using us as agents, God seeks to express His qualities and glory for the joy of experiencing Himself for what He conceptually knew Himself to be.

Before its discovery, electricity was nothing unto itself, until the Spirit within a man imagined and developed a method on how to generate, transmit, distribute and experience the power of electricity. Thomas Edison then imagined and developed an incandescent bulb as a means through which electrical light can be expressed and experienced. Then the Spirit worked within another man to imagine and develop a stove and a fridge as a medium through which the power of electricity could be expressed, utilized and experienced. Now we can flip a switch and flood a dark room with light or utilize a stove and fridge to preserve and prepare our food. The luxury of the lives we live today goes mostly unnoticed but lies within the intuition of the Spirit.

The Spirit within us is full of infinite possibilities. By focusing our attention on the desires, we seek to manifest, we can mold the formless, spiritual possibilities into their physical equivalent. Through imagining, the Spirit makes things out of itself. The Wright brothers thought of a machine that would travel through air, and they were given the means to create their spiritual prototype into its physical equivalent. If we focus and impress our desires upon the Spirit within us, we can also clothe our desires and transport them into this physical world.

The Spirit within you, who wears the garment of flesh and blood that is you, is forevermore seeking to express Itself through your body. It waits on you to pin-point the exact manner in which you would like It to express Itself, and therefore, you must know with definite precision what it is that you *would love to be and do.*

To allow the expression of this Spirit or the Father, a man must know *what he would love to be and do.* For we are told that, "I am the vine, you are the branches; he who abides in Me and I in him, he bears much fruit, for apart from Me you can do nothing. If anyone does not remain in Me, he is like a branch that is thrown away and withers. Such branches are gathered up, thrown into the fire, and burned." The man who does not know what he would love to be would become like a branch that withers and falls to the ground due to a lack of sap's supply from the vine, which will result in him being picked up by (fellow man), or the hands of life and be tossed aimlessly about. For If a man does not allow that which is within him to express itself through him, he will no longer act from a place of inspiration. And will go through life aimlessly and focus his energy on little things, thinking these accessories will bring him satisfaction, just to later realize that he never lived life as he longed to. We must allow that which is within us to express itself, for apart from that, we can do nothing but sell our soul and go through life purposeless and unsatisfied.

In the same manner as a branch allows and carries water and nutrients from the vein to give life to the fruits which it bears, a man must allow that which is within him to fully express its true self through his ideal.

There is something within every man, a Life-Force seeking fuller expanded expression of itself through a means of itself. It is solely for this purpose; that we are, that humanity is – that creation is. This is solely why there will always be longing and discontentment within our hearts when we are suppressing, denying, resisting this Thing within us and playing a superficial game in life and selling ourselves short. This thing is the voice of the Spirit, whispering to us, 'Grow! Grow more!' 'There is more for you'! For we are meant to be great. We have come from Greatness, and consequently, there is greatness within us seeking to reveal itself.

This Thing within us appears to be ghost-like. It will haunt you until you become attentive to it, and if you don't, you will drag your body through life unsatisfied, until you claim your place at the graveyard. What is within you is not scratching and eating you up on the inside and haunting you to make you feel heavy and unsatisfied in life, but solely because It wants you to remember it. It is seeking to express itself through you. For that is the basis of your creation. Thus, "My Father is glorified by this, that you bear much fruit…" Apart from *bearing much fruit*, our deeds become nothing but unfortunate.

We enjoy the fruits of those who came before us, who refused to accept things as they were, and dared to dream by producing new inventions and refining the existing ones for our comfort, benefit, convenience and the advancement of life. Yet we fail to dream and make a meaningful social contribution to humanity. We diminish a great and infinite power within us and would rather focus our efforts on small and unvalued tasks of acquiring materials things for ourselves. Horace Mann said, "We should be ashamed to die until we have made some major contribution to human kind." Our essence is a livingness of the Spirit, and the Spirit cannot be satisfied by the dusty accessories of life. We will never quench the thirst of the soul by drinking from a bottle of something, or by eating a mass of food, or by clothing ourselves in beautiful dresses and fine suits, or by touring the Bahamas. We can only satisfy and quench the soul's hunger and thirst by sharing the bread and wine within us with our fellow men and allow them to feast and drink abundantly from our life's work.

"We push and elbow our way through life and frantically struggle to get hold of things which we believe will make us happy, -and behold, the moment we grasp them, the charm, with which our imagination had invested them, vanishes!

The shallow things we had set our heart on yesterday are not the same things we yearn for today. They do not give the pleasure which was promised, and we are no nearer to satisfaction than before. Our attention is quickly attracted to something else, which we feel surely will compensate for our disappointment, and we grasp at it only to repeat the same experience – disappointment, and disillusionment. It does not fill the void in our hearts.

There is ever an unsatisfied longing which we spend our lives trying to fill. No matter what we may obtain in the way of material things, while we may get a certain sort of pleasure and comfort from them, they do not satisfy the inward soul hunger." We do not inhabit the earth to accumulate staff.

The Spirit of life is; and forever will be present within us, as is said, "I will never desert you, nor will I ever forsake you." The Spirit must flow through us in order to express itself, and it is paramount to know that, as in the laws and usage of electricity where we provide an electrical system with a load through which electricity can express itself, so must we in like manner provide the

Spirit within us with the correct channel through which it can express itself.

Within you is a genius that lies dormant and is waiting to be called upon. There is an ever-present Infinite Grid of power and intelligence; an Internal Creator, a Power intoxicated with a livingness of thought and feeling seeking to breathe life, gives form to the images you choose to impress upon your mind. These images can become real if lifted by us; they can become real for you, for your joy, for your happiness and fulfillment. This power can be likened to a well of infinite water running deep, that never dries up, and all that is required is for you to become aware and draw from this Power as you work towards that which you are called to be and do. But, you can only draw from it without much resistance and effort if you remember and become with Who You Really Are.

A man's foremost urge should be the endeavor to find his real-self, *'who he is'* and then the mode through which the his real-self can spring forth; whether he is to become an author, musician, inventor, or an entrepreneur. In whatsoever form his godly cry seeks expression itself, that is the calling. And through our feelings this we will be told.

Feelings Are Our Internal Guiding Systems

The Divine Spirit is all knowing – it knows all the truth there is, and therefore only the Divine-Spirit within us has real wisdom in helping us to do truthful and loving things at any given time. It whispers this to us through feelings, for feelings are the voice and language of the soul, and we will know the truth about anything in life by the way we feel towards and about that something. Feelings are our internal guiding system, forevermore seeking to keep us on the right path, the divine path, the path of our truth, whispering the truth to us so we can make the best decisions to be and do the right thing. There's a divine guidance and you will come to know it through a vibe, a sense of feeling within you that whispers to you that you need to do this thing or that thing. It is an inner light impelling you towards whatever is true, towards the noble thing, the right thing, the pure thing, the lovely thing, the greatest act, and so the highest fulfillment.

You shall come to know that you are on the right path, when everything you do is life giving and not life draining.

There is a feeling in every man, a feeling of knowing what to be and what to do, but he does not choose to follow this knowing and do what he knows he ought to do, for he is constantly being taught to ignore this feeling and follow practical logic. His intuition is silently screaming at him, but the demand of the day, society, and life distractions are pulling his mind in a million different directions, programming and encouraging him not to listen to his heart. Society and the corporate world tells him to stop thinking, to stop being creative, to stop being god and goddess, to stop being himself, suppressing the feeling within him, prompting him to walk away from the pathway he is to walk and abandon the service he is to render.

If you neglect to listen to your feeling and seek not to follow it, you will become submissive to other people's ideas and suggestions of what you should be and do, and you will never know what you are capable of. This will result in you not doing anything outside of your comfort zone or of great significance in life and you will never taste the yoke of fulfillment that you so know is your birth right.

Not only does the Divine Spirit seek to guide us to do the right thing that is in alignment with and true towards our vision, it also has within it the ability to inform us when we are off course and out of alignment with what we are called to be and do.

Your highest expression is creativity, and out of the well of your creative work, these qualities; love and beauty, magnificent, inspiration, kindness, compassion, fulfilment and advancement of life, must spring forth into the world, and for as long as we are not experiencing and expressing these qualities through that which we choose to be and through the work we are doing, then we are off-course and out of alignment with Who We Really Are. Through the emotion of uneasiness, unhappiness, anxiety, doubt, and worry, we will come to know that we are being and doing the wrong thing.

You will come to know all this by merely feeling bad about the work you are doing and longing for more, feeling frustrated in the space you occupy. Through a bad feeling, the Divine Spirit hereby reminds us we are off course and out of alignment, and our life expression will be bland and boring and feel like hell. We will feel as if everything in life is working against us. Through this, you will come to know that you are on the wrong path.

In your heart of hearts, if you are being something you are not born to be, you will know. If you are doing what you don't want, you will know. If things are not to your liking, if you are at a place where you are not supposed to be, where your spirit has long left, you will know.

But no matter the circumstances or the situation you find yourself in, there is but one thing no man can take away from you, and that is your choice. You have a choice to limit yourself or to choose to grow, to put your focus on the circumstances, (the boisterous winds) and sink, or on your desire (Jesus) and walk fearlessly towards it. You have free will to either listen to the external deceiving voices, or your inner-self whispers and choose to walk the path that you know is rightfully yours even if the rest of the world disagrees with you.

You Are Adam And Eve

The Bible is purely spiritual and psychological, a book about the inner activities in the mind of man, rather than a book of theology. The mere fact that it is still relevant today and enjoys a prestige status is proof that it is not a book to be taken for history but as a guide that refers to the psychological challenges man faces in his mind and the choices he ought to make every day as he navigates through life. Only the foolish man will take it literally; any intelligent man who in all he seeks, seeks wisdom, will understand that the Bible is written in idiomatic, philosophical language; he will understand and, rightfully so, that the Bible uses external activities to portray inner psychological and spiritual truths, in an attempt to make him understand that the game of life is all psychological and the power and choice lies within him and not outside him.

The game of life is twofold. A choice between love or fear. A choice between life and death, prosperity and adversity. Hence, we are told, "… I have set before you life and death, the blessing and the curse. So, choose life in order that you may live…"

The story of life and the way for the individual who walks the face of the earth is contained in the story of the Garden of Eden. It is a story recorded not to present men with a historical drama, but to convey a life gospel. In the religious circles, the Bible is often referred to as the *book of life*; not a historical book, or of geography, but of life, the present life, the only life that is now. So, the drama that is recorded in the Bible is unfolding right now in the mind of man.

No intelligent man will take the story of Adam and Eve in the Garden of Eden literally. Who among man is so foolish to think that the All-Knowing God must have planted a tree of the knowledge of good and evil like a garden keeper, created a man in Adam and Eve, together with 'deceiving entity' that appeared in the form of a serpent, and put all these creatures in the same garden? As if God was somehow and secretly plotting for the downfall of Adam and Eve? Unless if we are mocking God, the architect of the Universe, Him who sustains life. The battle of Adam and Eve, is our battle even to this day – it is psychological.

We must thus proceed to realize that, in this drama, there are two voices within us. A voice of truth from a Higher Power, as represented by the Lord. This is our inner voice, our intuition constantly telling us to do the right thing and which way to go, whispering this information through our own feelings. And then there is always the voice of reason, the logical mind as represented by the *serpent*, reasoning with us (as represented Eve), countering the truth as told to us by the voice of truth, which is our intuition, the Higher Power. The *voice of reason* always seeks to counter this *voice of truth*, all in attempt to deceive and lead us astray. It appears that if we don't trust and follow the guidance of our intuition or Higher Power, we are likely to submit to the suggestions of the deceitful-voices (as represented by the serpent), bad advice and limiting beliefs from fellow men, do the wrong thing, take the wrong path, perish, and surely be led to the death of our souls.

We will be met and presented with deceiving and tempting things, especially from the external. But we have a choice to obey and honor our intuition, the still voice of truth and walk the path of faith, listening to a voice that will lead us on a path to where we are going to taste the richness of life. We also have a choice to choose fear, to listen to a deceiving voice that will limit us and make us remain stagnant in life.

Many a man are constantly accepting deceitful suggestions and limiting believes from fellow man, and they then become fearful and thus are led to the death of their souls by doing things they don't want to do and feeling empty and unfulfilled.

Be courageous and follow your heart and your intuition. You do not have to know how you can live out your vision. Within your mind is a faculty that will show you the way – your wonderful human imagination. So, trust your vision.

Live Fully or Sell Your Soul and Die

Adversity in the life of the individual is inevitable, and there comes a time in life where a man will meet adversity sometimes unbeknown and in his own unique way. It will be a period of darkness, a period of hardship, a time in life where he meets a new experience that is not so lovely, where he is forced to hit rock bottom and taste failure, pain and suffering; either physically, emotionally, spiritually or otherwise – this he cannot escape for as-long as he travels the face of the earth in the envelope of the soul dipped in blood in his mother's womb.

A man is either born in a dire environment, an upbringing rooted in pain that he faces right out of his mother's womb, or he will face a sad period later in the journey of life, where he will lose a parent or loved one while young or old, or where he will have a devastating heartbreak from a relationship, such as a divorce. Indeed, a time will present itself in life where a man will practically lose everything; a job, a house, fall deeper into debt, or a devastating car accident that will change the course of his life for good; or a time where all his attempts to improve his life seem to be in vain, and that some invisible forces of the world are against his every effort, driving him deeper into a pit of discouragement and struggle.

But in all the hardship and pain we ever encounter, the choice remains within us to arise or to remain in the tomb, to live or to die. We can either let our adversities crush us or use them to raise us to new heights. There is always a small window of decision making when we are faced with some difficulties: a choice to choose life or to choose death, not death in physical form, but the death of our soul, to die silently on the inside, to rusts and corrode within, to give up on seeking the life we desire, to not go after our dreams, our vision, or to not live out our calling. We all have stories, and we have a choice to entertain and feed the sad and painful part of our stories, or chose to shed them and move forward, focusing on our strength and what we are good at, and utilize that to propel us further as we pursue to express the highest version of who we are.

We must cut through the invisible cages that seem to inhabit us, through the thick mud that seems to want to hold us in the dirt. As the plants grow out of the dirt of the earth, utilizing the dirt as the foundation, extracting only the elements which they need for their growth from the soil to bear the fruit they will, so may a man also uses his source of suffering, (his seemingly dirt) as the source and the foundation of his success. The same way as the resources for the growth of the plant lies within the tip of its roots, so lies within man's reach (and through asking the right questions) the answers and tools that can he can utilize to put him towards a path that will make him become the best him, making him grow, expand, and express himself in his full glory.

The mystery hidden in the dreadful death of the son of Mary is a call for us to arise. To arise out of our miseries, out of our pain and struggle, and out of our sad experiences. For within us is an everlasting power that cannot even be stopped, contained and limited by the strongest of tombs.

Those who crucified Jesus represent a condition, a period, or a circumstance that we find ourselves in that is threatening to bury us in the tomb of adversity, suffering, and struggle. Circumstances might appear and seemingly empower us and get the better of us, and place a heavy stone on us, but let it be for two days, and on the 3rd day you have to arise and return to your Father, to Who You Really Are, because you are an eternal being.

If Divine-Spirit is All-knowing and knew you while you were in your mother's womb, and ordained you a prophet unto his nation, then he too must have known the dire environment and hardship you will enter and face upon your birth. God must have known, too, the circumstances you will face as a young and untested soul. He must have known and lined up the souls that will guide and set you on your path, and yet he allowed you to be born in the very environment and to face the very pressing and unwanted circumstances you have faced. For God knows that that which is within you is far greater than anything in this world.

As a soldier needs sufficient and certain training before sending him to a battlefield and every astronaut is fully equipped with all the necessary clothing in order to live in the condition he is to face in that world, so God places environment and circumstances as mere tools and training to shape and mold you for that which you are called to do in life.

The very source of your suffering and pain could be the very source of your success and freedom, if you could but stop judging and cursing your not-so-good experiences, and rather try to lean into them and listen. There is always a message that is rightfully ours, that if understood could set us on a new grander path that will change our life like night and day. Thus, helping us not sell our soul and die, but assist us to live fully.

Find out WHO You Really Are and,
be WHO You Really Are and,
share WHO You Really Are with the world
In WHAT-so-ever manner you would love.

CHAPTER 2
WHAT?

What you are here for

The meaning of life is to find your gift.
The purpose of life is to give it away.
–Pablo Picasso

Trust the Vision Within Your Soul

Every man faces one significant question:" *What* am I here for?"

As an individual, it is every man's function to be somebody and to do something of significance and worthwhile to the advancement and betterment of life itself, to live fully, to express his fullest potential, and to be the best possible him. However, this potential can only be expressed along a certain pattern. Like an architectural building-blueprint along which a building is erected, every man has a certain pattern of growth, and it is easier for him to grow in alignment with his unique pattern than along any other lines of growth. He is given certain talents and gifts that enables him to grow easier in a certain pattern than along any other pattern. Together with this pattern, man is connected to an infinite grid of intelligence that he can naturally encourage to aid him ones he starts moving along his distinct pattern of growth.

> *"What we all want is to be able to live out the truest, highest expression of ourselves." –Oprah Winfrey*

This unique pattern of growth can only be realized through the path of *being-ness*. By being Who You Really Are, by walking the path of your true design, the path of your calling, doing your life's work. By being thyself, Then you can *do* what you are called to do. For being-ness gives birth and also fuels *doing-ness*, and if implemented in that order produces *having-ness,* (to have all the accessories in life that you desire). That is the paradigm (!) and the secret to life, for (having-ness) or accumulating things in life does not produce (being-ness) or fulfilment and happiness.

If you truly want to be happy, you have to be you. Not the 'you' your parents and friends want or expect you to be, or the 'you' circumstances or the educational system has forced and molded you to become, or the 'you' society expects you to become. Only you know Who You Really Are, and what you would love to be and do. "For who among men knows the thoughts of a man, except the spirit of the man which is in him?" The innermost purpose known only to the self is what brings you life, and you must pursue it without ceasing.

There is something that you have that nobody else has: you. You are already taken by 'you' and no one can occupy the form that is 'you'. Your story, your experiences, your way of being, your way of doing things, your way of thinking, your voice, this are all well compounded elements for the expression of your own unique light.

Wallace D. Wattles knew this to be true when he said, "Upon growth, one person may become a rose and add brightness and colour to some dark corner of the world. One person may be a lily and teach a lesson of love and purity to everyone. Another person may be a climbing vine and hide the rugged outlines of some dark rock. And yet another person may be a great oak among whose boughs the birds shall nest and sing." Martin Luther King, in a similar vein, encouraged and said, "It isn't by the size that you win or fail …be a bush if you can't be a tree. If you can't be a highway, be a trail. If you can't be the sun, be a star – but be the best of whatever you are."

"The two most important days in your life are the day you are born and the day you find out why."
–Mark Twain

Then the question arises, how is a man to find this thing that is planted inside of him, the knowledge of which will change everything? How shall he know the one life giving thing he is to express, the expression of which will make him taste the sweet nectar and richness of life. How shall he know that he is to be a bush, or a tree, or a lily, or a rose and add colour and brightness to some dark corner of the world?

I should submit to you upfront that the knowledge of this is important but not difficult. The most pressing challenge that is facing humanity the world over is the temerity to follow and live out this thing once it is known.

Somewhere in his gut and heart of hearts, every man has a suspicion about the service he wants to render. There is a whisper of this, a knowing, a gentle confirmation deep within you of the work you are to do. You shall know this thing for you will notice it in your actions and through the things that draw you. In your noble pursuits and personal endeavours, you will be attracted to mostly the things that resonate with Who You Are. Some of them will become your obsession, for birds of a feather flock together, and life will push, pull, and guide you to circumstance, events and people in a silent and unnoticeable manner, all in attempts to remind you of your self – all these as mere symbols, having one message for you: "This is the work you are to do, this is Who You Are."

Tom Bilyeu's words also bring us closer to this thing when he said, "Inside of you, based on the things you have encountered in your life, there are certain areas of interest, and by engaging with this area of interest, you will discover there is something that you are legitimately fascinated by, capturing your attention."

If you have but the ears to hear and the eyes to see, and a heart to feel, then through feelings you will know the thing you want to be and do, for it will come to you through silence and calm. An absolute knowing will find home in your heart of hearts of the very thing you are to be and do; don't turn your attention from it, don't rationalize it, but rather just listen, trust, and follow it fearlessly.

There is no doubt in my mind that the Creator of the universe could have orchestrated it entirely different to what it is today. The manner in which the world appears to the mortal senses and the harmonious manner in which the world and the planets function is proof beyond literacy and rationality that the world was deliberately orchestrated to exist in the exact manner as it exists. The way the rain falls, the way the wind blows, the manner in which the earth revolves around the sun, all this deliberate behavior as we have come to witness, could not have come into play by mere happenstance. Although no man can touch this invisible intelligence behind all creation with a finger, we can all acknowledge its existence and presence through the external comportment exhibited by nature. Through the deliberate and harmonious cooperation displayed by the planets, from the external demeanor of the galaxies, we can witness that it truly exists, even just by staring at the external beauty of a lotus flower; the love, the peace, beauty it exhibits. From this, we can conclude with absolute conviction that the world and all creation was erected along a certain blueprint – a deliberate pattern. So, this Creator must have at some period in its existence had a *clear vision* for the world and so a certain pattern of growth and play for each and every thing which it longed to create.

We also have come to know that there is no man-made thing in this world that came into being without the formless prototype of the thing not first having flashed as an image (or a vision) in the mind of man. This method through which things materialize in the world of the individual, through which man has brought his desires in his own world since the beginning of time must only have been inherited from his own Creator, since we are told that man was created in the image and likeness of his Creator.

The point I am trying to bring across is that Spirit seeks or embodies the focused thought or vision that the mind has conceived. That is the law in creation, and as spiritual beings having a human experience, if we seek to create a thing, we are only to align ourselves with the law and modus operandi of Spirit. Therefore, we must embrace and honor the **vision** shown to us by the Spirit within us, by this Invisible Intelligence within us, showing us our own unique pattern of growth.

Hence we are told, **"Where there is no vision, the people perish: but he that keepeth the law, happy is he."**

Not that people will perish and never find their way back home (for consciousness is not eternally ignorant), but until they remember Who They Really Are, they will perish. Perish they will; for not having a vision, for not keeping the law, by not growing within their own unique pattern of expression. They will perish by not living fully to their fullest potential, by not stretching and becoming their grandest version of who they know themselves to be – perish by blending in destruction and leading a meaningless life and by ceasing to flourish, making little or no contribution to the betterment and advancement of life and that of humanity. If a man follows this narrative, he will perish and be used by those with a vision to help them build theirs on his back, for he lacks the courage to follow his own. he will perish by doing jobs that he loathes, hovering from one mundane job to another, living pay-cheque to pay-cheque just to put bread and butter on his table. This is what he will amount to, by becoming a begging and fearful soul. But if he is to be happy, fulfilled, and free, he ought to keep the law. And the law is to trust and follow the vision that has been planted inside of his soul, to be himself. The man that aligns himself with the law, who decides on a crystal-clear vision for himself, who seeks his own unique pattern of self-expression, he is sure to meet untold prosperity and true freedom.

This truth has been proven times without number by those who came before us, by the thought and business leaders who against all odds decided to live out the vision planted in their soul. This law was kept by the son of Mary to the letter. Jesus, who by living out his vision, or what he often referred to as 'the will of his father' gave birth to a revolution that has manifested itself far and wide into every household across the globe, even in the forgotten parts of the world.

You will become as great as your dominant aspiration….
If you cherish a vision, a lofty ideal in your heart, you
will realize it. –James Allen

You are here because something has called you into being, for a divine mission. And you are endowed with the power, ability and all the tools to fulfil this mission. You are here to resurrect and bring to life a thought, a desire, a vision – the image in your heart.

But no man knows your purpose; this is why Jesus said, "All things have been entrusted to Me by My Father. No one knows the Son save the Father, and no one knows the Father save the Son and those to whom the Son chooses to reveal Him."

The above statement contains a world of wisdom and If we are to express this philosophical statement in simple a language we are to say: 'The work you are to do has been entrusted to you by your Father. '…No one knows this vision except yourself and those to whom you choose to reveal this vision.'

No one knows your inner-most thoughts, the thoughts that drops silently within you, but yourself, and those to whom you choose to reveal these thoughts.

There is a unique calling on your life that you do not get to ignore. It is the very thing that you long to express in this world, and that you know will bring joy to your soul. It is the change you wish to see in the world. Your calling is not out of reach, but rather right under your nose, for it is a child born of your upbringing and background, of your environment, your challenges and experiences, both good and bad, especially the seemingly bad. All this are but the tools utilized by God to shape, mold and build your character and to equip you with the necessary education and training so you may carry out the work you are called to do. The wounds of the seemingly bad experiences that have stuck and seems to follow you where ever you go in this world, are but your foundation upon which you will build your castle, for they have empowered you with resilience, determination and resourcefulness. They are the ground upon which the plane that is you will take off and fly high into the ether where freedom, fulfilment and peace dwells.

This child that is your calling belongs less to you than to those who will be inspired by it. To die without expressing what you long to express is to rob life of a precious remedy that is intended to quench, feed and heal hundreds of thousands and possibly millions of people around the world. Do not deny your Father's work, for it is about the betterment and advancement of life, your life is not about you, the individual, it is about the whole. For, "Life is a process that teaches and informs life about life through the process of life itself", and so through you as an integral component of life itself, life seeks to teach life, to heal life and informs life.

I like the words of Lisa Nichols. They are words of an awakened soul. They are spoken out of a full life of rich experience and wisdom. They are one of the most beautiful truths I have always known and am in constant need of reminder.

As Nichols said, "If no one in your family gets your vision; if your wife doesn't get it, if your husband doesn't get it, if your partner does not get it, if your children don't get it; your parents or your siblings or your friends, if no one gets your vision, hear me when I say; It is because God did not give it to them; God gave your vision to you. And it is your job to birth it, to nurture it, it's your job to grow it, so that the rest of the world can enjoy it, your job is to be obedient to your calling."

Greatness is not reserved for the select few; it is in every living man. There might be great men we admire and idolize, and we may think that they are different and perhaps a rare breed. But they are man of flesh and blood just like us, bleeding the same red blood, and just like me and you, they all came out of the womb in the nude, speechless and with their eyes closed. We all drink the same water and we all breathe the very same air. No man of flesh and blood has more greatness within him than anyone else. Whether they are from the east or from the west, all men are subjected to the same laws on earth. The only difference between man is the level of awareness and expression of Who They Really Are.

The magnitude of expression of electrical current can be restricted and allowed differently in various parts of the world, but the power of electricity itself and the laws that governs it are the same in every part of the world. In much the same way the Life-Force seeking expression through every man is the same within every living human being, wherever nature has located him, but the difference is that some men tend to do greater things than others because they have found the pattern of their own unique self-expression - thus allowing more of this Life-Force to flow through them.

Every successful man is where he is, doing what he does, and having what he has solely because he has sought and found who he really is. No man came to planet earth all-knowing. Every successful man has to realize their personal calling, and act upon it. Because we all came into the world knowing nothing, any man can become that which he would love to be, and do what he would love to do, and have what he would love to have, if he puts his mind to it. No man should allow another man of flesh and blood to make him feel less capable, for all men are infinitely great. The eternal truth is that there is always something that one man can do better than the other. If we were to force musicians and singers to design architectural blueprints and judge them accordingly, they would live their lives thinking they are worthless. If we were to force accountants construct houses, then they would live their whole lives thinking they are useless. As Albert Einstein said, "Everybody is a genius. But if you judge a fish by its ability to climb a tree, it will live its whole life believing that it is stupid."

Throughout this book, I have chiefly emphasized being-ness and doing-ness, and less so on having-ness, for having-ness happens automatically once the first two paradigms are applied. In the moment that you start being what you would love to be, and doing the things you would love to do, the things you would love to have are self-regulating. I can without hesitation prove the above statement, for it is recorded in scripture, "...and every branch that bears fruit, He prunes it so that it may bear more fruit", or even more profoundly, "but seek first His kingdom and His righteousness, and all these things will be added to you."

I must, however, hasten here to add and bring clarity to this much-misinterpreted verse. The kingdom we must seek is not a terrestrial kingdom of silver and gold that men on the earth have fashioned. Jesus never taught or recognized such a kingdom, for there is no true kingdom of the kind. It is sad and unfortunate that we have been brought up to believe that heaven is a place that cannot be enjoyed on earth, but that it is only through the path of death that we can experience it. Yet the prayer of Jesus leaves us not in ambiguity. He wouldn't have demanded the kingdom of his 'our Father' to come on earth, if it was a terrestrial place that is to be occupied after this life.

"Our Father who art in Heaven

Thy kingdom come...on earth as it is in Heaven" and, also,

"Neither shall they say, Lo here! or, lo there! for, behold, the kingdom of God is within you."

"We carry within us the wonders
we seek without us" –Browning

The kingdom that is referred to in the scripture is the very light you are to express in this world, the thing you are to be and do. It is your life's work. *'And his righteousness'* means to live with integrity and in alignment with who you really are, to live in harmony with one's essence and to allow the expression of the thing seeking to express itself through us. This is the true kingdom referred to in the scripture that we must aim for. This is the eternal, priceless gem of truth that will set you free.

A man can be, do, and have anything he would love to; be it a leader, actor, business man, or whatever it is that he would love. He must know what he would love to be and do and by always keeping the paradigm in this order: *be, do, and* then *have*. If you wish to verify the truth in these message, look up to the world-renowned singers, entrepreneurs, the actors and actresses. You cannot help but witness that success, abundance, and true freedom comes if you are being and doing that which you are called to be and do, without falling victim to the influence of the world around us. This is the modus operandi of the law of the universe. The key to your success solely rests in you embodying your life's purpose and true calling. God has placed within you all the intelligence and resources you will ever need to accomplish your dream. All the wisdom you ever need is inside of you.

'Seek ye first the kingdom of God' does not mean to first secure your spot of eternal rest in a mortal kingdom of gold and silver after life on earth through repentance, as if a place of that nature exists. When that is the mindset, we tend to go through life thinking we will be greatly rewarded for our selfish acts of repenting and idling. It is our eternal refusal to seek the true message and to validate the truth of these scriptures, and our proneness to substitute them with our own made up meanings, that have ushered in the bareness that is so evident in the everyday life of believers. As such, we have yet to witness the promise of, "Let your light shine before men in such a way that they may see your good works, and glorify your Father who is in heaven," in their lives.

God is forevermore seeking fuller expanded expression of his kingdom that is within our midst. There is no place of idling and eternal rest called heaven that has been advertised and that is being fashioned, for the Father who art in heaven has embarked upon a journey seeking to express his kingdom. This means he will forevermore be seeking to express his kingdom through you as you, even after this life, and into infinity.

Les Brown once said, "The graveyard is the richest place on earth, because it is here that you will find all the hopes and dreams that were never fulfilled, the books that were never written, the songs that were never sung, the inventions that were never shared, the cures that were never discovered, all because someone was too afraid to take that first step, keep with the problem, or determined to carry out their dream."

While there is an element of truth in the words of Les, I am afraid I would like to whisper to him the words of the Nazarene, "Let the dead bury the dead." For before we even get to the graveyard, there is another place that is far richer than all the graveyards on the entire planet earth combined. It is the living souls walking on the surface of the earth itself. In truth, it is the living who are working against the Creative Power of the universe, rather than with it.

If there is anyone who needs awakening and inspiration, it is us, the living, who are afraid to take the necessary steps required to walk towards our dreams. It is us, the living, who are not persistent enough to carry out our dreams. It is us, the living, who never attempt to step out and walk away from comfort. It is us, the living, who do not believe there is greatness within us, who do not believe we can take a dream and give it form by breathing life into its nostrils with the power within us. It is us who have eaten the fruit from the tree of knowledge just to use it for idleness rather than striving. In turn, we have been driven out from the garden of inspiration and sent to a death of idleness and hopelessness. If there is anyone who needs lecture, it is us, the living, who think circumstances and conditions have so great a power over us that we are incapable of change. If there is anyone who needs awakening, it is the living who are not aware that we have dominion over circumstances in this world of matter.

The words "seek his face!" means to seek the face of the spiritual-expression knocking in our hearts, not a face of a mortal being, but the face of the vision placed within us, seeking to express itself through us. Get to know it, and befriend it. Decision, faith, and action are a child born of knowing exactly what you would love to be and do. By having a definite purpose, you will start to create your future self in advance, for you will start clothing your idea in the soil of your mind, and you will be able to see your ideal self and your ideal future. Once you can visualize your ideal life, you will soon come to know that you will blend right into your ideal future in the upcoming days, and you will experience the bliss of what you imagine.

Hold and cherish what you would love to be and do, long enough for it to become part of your identity. Once it has become part of your identity, you will begin to feel in your heart that it is so, and soon, you will start to render to yourself, in silence, the song of King David, "…though I walk through the valley of the shadow of death, I will fear no evil."

Hold the end in mind; hold fast to your vision with all the tenacity you can muster, and you will have called the creative power within you from the deep to come on board on your journey. Holding the end in mind will generate the motive for action, and by acting you will attract the ideas, information, events, and people that will assist you in attaining your desire.

However, it is undeniable that like every other successful man, you will confront hardships and face challenges. But no matter the magnitude of the challenges and circumstances met along the way, knowing what you want to be and do, deposits within the heart a silent knowing that challenges come to pass and not to stay. For circumstances are not a permanent truth; the truth is the Life-Spirit and the divine dream within us. They know that the circumstances will soon set them free, for it cannot hold unto them for too long, for they are a child of another environment where excellence, success and freedom dwells.

Patanjali knew this when he said, "When you are inspired by some great purpose, some extraordinary project, all your thoughts break their bonds: Your mind transcends limitations, your consciousness expands in every direction, and you find yourself in a new, great and wonderful world. Dormant forces, faculties and talents become alive, and you discover yourself to be a greater person by far than you ever dreamed yourself to be."

We are told a great story of Peter and Jesus that unfolded at the lake of Galilea in the scripture. Now in this drama, Jesus means your *'dream'* or the *'thing that you would love to be, do and have'*. He is your saviour, because your dream or that which you would love to be, do, and have is your saviour. For it will bring you freedom, influence, abundance, success, fulfilment, and everything else that you would love to experience if you attain it. Peter means '*faith*' and '*perseverance*'. The boisterous wind represents '*fear*' which will appear in various forms, like you conditioning your dream, the challenges, old paradigm trying to keep you at the same place, your own negative stories and excuses, obstacles and the negative opinion of friends, parents and other fellow man. The boat means your seemingly '*comfort zone*' and '*safety*'. The water means an *unfamiliar route or path* that we must walk on as we attempt to walk towards our desire.

You, as Peter, are called to walk towards your *dream or* the '*thing that you would love to be, do and have*' with faith. I said in the beginning of the chapter, we do not get to choose our dreams, but in fact our dreams choose us. It is, however, our job to seek and identify our dream, and ask our dream to command us to walk towards it through an unfamiliar route, thus, "Lord, if it is You, command me to come to You on the water." Now this is you as Peter, demanding to walk towards your dream after you have identified it. Your '*dream*' or the '*thing that you would love to be, do or have*," as represented by Jesus, is saying to you, "Come". Now this is your dream, calling you forth to step out of the boat and walk towards it, focusing solely on it.

In this seemingly historical drama, you are assured that the challenges and *fear* as represented by the boisterous winds will come. You are also assured that if, for a moment, you look at the *fear* (the boisterous wind), such as challenges, excuses, old paradigms, or obstacles, and you allow negative opinion of other men to rent a place in your mind, you will immediately oust your faith with fear and you are sure to sink.

We must project our attention and understanding on the sheer truth that, if we take a leap of faith like Peter did in the beginning, before he wavered after projecting his attention towards the boisterous wind, we will walk towards our dream, or the thing we would love to be, do, and have. We are also assured that our dream is our only true friend and saviour, for even if we sink, fail, or suffer defeat, and then recognize it again, it is there to stretch its hand and pick us up. "Immediately Jesus reached out His hand and took hold of Peter."

You must equip yourself with a garment of faith and concentrate your attention on your internal purpose, and never for a moment shift your focus. Let the wind blow, let the challenges arise, and let the opinion of other men be like water off, of a duck's back. Do not seek to entertain them, and you are sure to walk towards your dream and attain it.

If you persistently pursue and hold onto your dream, an absolute knowing is soon to find home within your heart. Once that happens, you will know that circumstances, excuses, obstacles, and opinions do not aid you in attaining that which you would love to be and do. Sooner or later, that negativity will crumble down like the walls of Jericho, and you will march into the beautiful city and claim what is yours. This process will earn you that which you would love to be, do, and have, for the wind of change within you will have blown down any barrier. No walls so high and thick, and no gates so tightly locked, will stop a man who knows what he would love to be, do, and have.

There is faith in knowing precisely what it is you want. For even as you walk through the valley of darkness, you shall fear nothing, for you know in your heart of hearts that your dream will eventually lead you to green pastures and still waters.

There are plans and opportunities contained within the desire itself, but the plans are self-inviting only for the man who knows what it is he is working towards. He may get stuck, but momentarily it will be. Even in that momentary delay, at least he knows what he would love to be and do, and because he knows this, he is quick to notice any good idea or opportunity that he can utilize to propel him in the direction of achieving his purpose.

The first path to true freedom and success is in an unwavering knowing of what you would love to be and do. Solely focus your mind on the purpose, and once that is figured out, the things you want will come naturally to you. In the same manner as the Lord feeds the birds, who do not sow or reap, nor gather into barns, so knows your Lord that you need to be fed, clothed and sheltered.

Therefore, you must solely focus on that which you would love to be, and in the meanwhile do the things you would love to do, as if you were already that which you would love to be. Then you can rest assured that your heavenly Father will give you shelter, feed you luxuriously, and clothe you as beautifully as the lilies, and more so than Solomon in all his glory.

There is an old saying, "No wind is favorable to the sailor who has no destination in mind." If you do not know where you are going, you will not know how to set the sails into the wind of Life. You will not know how to use the rudder; thus, you will not know how to guide your ship, that is the medium of your own Spirit.

We put bits into the mouths of the horses to make them obey us, and we guide the whole animal, but who is it that steers our body? Although driven by strong winds, the captain inclines the ships wherever it may go, by steering it with a very small rudder, but who is it that steers our body? Is it circumstances? Is it a lack of education? Is it the environment? Or is it that from which you have come from? It should be the latter, and that from which you originate from communicates with you through *intuition* as a mechanism to guide you towards your dream. The question is, are you listening?

Our only responsibility on our planet is to identify the thing that we would love to be and do, and then share it, by doing one deed wherever we are, and then the next, and so on. We can go about our daily affairs but must keep listening attentively to the voice of *intuition*, that small voice of truth, the voice of the Father. It is the voice of that from which you have come from, within you. It is the voice of guidance; and if heard and followed, it will not only take us to our destination, but to a place that

"No eye has seen, no ear has heard, and no mind has imagined…"

Know WHAT you would love to be, and
do the things you would love to do, and
the things you want to have will be given unto you;
but you have to know WHY you want to be and do what you
want to.

Muzire Mbuende – 2016

Chapter 3
Why?

You need a why

"If you want to lead a happy life –
tie it to a goal not to people or things"
– Albert Einstein

The most significant question that needs answering by every man is, "Why am I seeking to achieve this dream?"

Keeping your desires in alignment with who you really are requires you to know *why* you would love to be, do, or have whatever you dream of. Your 'why' is your biggest ally, and the factor that will enable you to cut through obstacles like a hot knife cutting through butter. It is the fuel that will keep you moving when the going gets tough and steep. You are a human being, and first and foremost, you are here to be. You are here to express and experience who you really are, and that is the core motive of why we have incarnated into this terrestrial world. Your soul seeks to experience what it knows itself to be, but most men are too focused on superficial things to recognize this, therefore abandoning their true purpose. Men are busy accumulating objects in the hope that eventually they may find time, money, and freedom, and then perhaps do the things they wish to do, and hopefully enjoy life. Instead, by the time they retire, they realize that they are physically and mentally exhausted, and cannot truly enjoy what they had worked so hard for. They then realize that they never utilized their time to be and do what they needed to for two-thirds of their life span and have entered their last phase of living on earth without truly having lived. It is therefore essential to know that no matter what your age, or where you are in life, you must know what you would love to be and do and start at once.

It is of paramount importance to know *why* you would love to be what you wish to be and do, and your intention of wanting to be and do must be bigger than your excuses and limiting beliefs. Your will must be bigger than your negative stories and thoughts; bigger than your lack of skills and knowledge, bigger than your unfavorable environment and conditions, and bigger than your circumstance or lack of education. If your intention is weaker than your excuses - that is, if you do not have a big enough 'why' - rest assured that your excuses and fear will crush your good intentions. Consequently, your excuses will suppress any seed of faith or courage you wish to entertain in your mind that would have helped you take the necessary steps to pursue your dreams, and you will thus be reduced to nothing but a begging soul that will constantly bow to the dictates of life and the opinions of other men.

Knowing the reasons one reaches for their dreams provides the motivation to become what you would love to be, have, or do, for it allows you to hold the end in mind. This in turn compels you not to waste your attention and energy by focusing it on the escape. You will view obstacles as peripheral additions, for your attention is fixed on what is vital (your dream), even in the midst of everything that opposes you. You will do everything in your power to achieve what you would love to achieve, for you know within your heart that you have a greater calling than anything that confronts you, and misrepresents the image of your desire. Man can turn you down, but in your soul, a waking angel stirs. This angel will be breathing words of inspiration into your mind. As you remind and motivate yourself with words of hope that "it is either my dream or nothing," and also employ that attitude, you will have called forth all the creative power from the deep to aid you in achieving your dream.

Desire and intention are the seedlings of all creations of good report. A man should abandon the idea of attempting to accumulate material things first, and then trying to be and do the things he loves after accumulating all the accessories he deems necessary. He will soon end up giving up his soul, and losing his integrity, for he will have used his physical and mental muscle to get frivolous things. It is lovely to get objects for enjoyment and to be comforted by them, but we should know there is no storage in heaven for all the things we are busy accumulating here on earth. This is why spending the better part of our life focusing on getting *things* is a path that has led many a man to go through life feeling empty in their souls.

A man should focus on being what he would love to *be*, and then doing the things he would love to do, and earning the things he would love to have, as they will, on their own, come to him. That is the method of working with the creative power of the universe, and a principle that will enable us to enjoy the journey as we seek to achieve our ideal life.

"Seek His kingdom, and all these things will be given to you" should be, 'seek to be and do the things which you were born to be and do, and the material things will be given to you.'

Life is about becoming, expressing, sharing, and experiencing. It is never about getting. It is about being and not about having, for it is in the process of being and sharing who we really are that a hundredfold is given unto us. This truth is plainly evident throughout Nature. All of life's natural creations are always seeking to serve other living organisms. The conduct of Nature is a message abundantly clear on how we should conduct ourselves in life: 'be the source'.

The trees, the grass, the sun, the rain, the beast on dry land, the fish in the ocean, and everything else in creation is in the process of feeding, providing, and sharing.

However, the highly conscious beings called humanity act differently, but in truth, our deeds should be no differently aligned than the deeds of the least conscious creations on the earth.

Nature, through its own way of being, has shown us that whatever we would love to be and do must be universally beneficial, to serve and bless others in one way or another. Our ideals should be achieved creatively and with the intention to give more to others, and we need to cast aside the destructive and competitive behaviour we have keenly employed in life so far by attempting to accumulate the *things* we want think we make us happy, sometimes by all means possible. We are enough. Indeed, everyone is enough, because the very Spirit that gives life to every individualized branch is enough, and abundant unto itself.

Again, it is imperative that your vision, or that which you would love to be and do, is mainly to serve others, both the current world and for generations unborn. It should not be a self-serving course, trying to take care of oneself, or to feed your children luxuriously, or to take good care of your family and relatives. These are obvious responsibilities, but are peripheral and limited. If a man minimizes his goals to these acts, he in turn limits God, and limits the very Infinite-Spirit that is seeking to express itself through him. What is paramount on the earth is the ability to serve others abundantly with your God given gifts, in whatever form you think is best to embody them. The medium or the genre of which you choose to serve others is of little significance. What matters is that it is done solely with the purpose to serve.

It is through the process of doing more that we tend to receive more. The more people a man serves, the more his return. The more corn seeds he sows, the more corn-kernels he will harvest, and the more barns he will fill. If we invest and bury more in the earth, the earth will return more unto us. This is a given consequence, because of the law of cause and effect. Thus we are told, "A gift opens the way and ushers the giver into the presence of the great."

Consider the scripture statement, "A man reaps what he sows." A rather negative connotation is associated with this great statement which bears with it one of life's greatest secrets of all times. It is understandable, since the statement is prone to be attached to both the negative and positive conduct of man. On the other hand, this statement hides a profound gem of truth and a great secret. For if what you are sowing is for the highest good of many, a sevenfold will be returned unto you. If you are sowing kindness into the hearts of a hundred, or a thousand, you can now judge for yourself how much kindness you will receive in return. Show compassion and love, enlighten your people, provide a good service or a good product to hundreds of thousands, and you can see that the return will only be a matter of exponents.

Therefore, you must know what you would love to be and do, and why. If you can execute that which you seek to be and do, your good will cannot help but come back to you in one form or another. It is a metaphysical law.

The thing that you would love to '*be*' will come to you through the process of you embodying and becoming the very thing that you would love to '*be*' right now. The things that you would love to '*do*' will come to you through the process of you *doing* the things you would love to *do* right now. Then the things you would love to have will be given unto you a hundredfold.

We are told in scripture that, "In the beginning was the Word, and the Word was with God, and the Word was God." And then, "...the Word became flesh, and dwelt among us..."

The point worthy of your attention in this scripture is *"the word was God"*, meaning one cannot separate God from the Word, nor the Word from God. It is One-Thing. So, our noble desires and intentions are truthfully God Himself, seeking to express Himself by becoming the very desire we have imagined. The Spirit makes things out of itself, and since we are mediums of Spirit, we use the same creative power and method to manifest into our visible world the thing which is planted in the womb of our mind. The Spirit truly becomes in the land of time and space the thing we have conceived in our mind.

So, a man has to know what and '*why*' he would love to be the thing which he would love to be. That's the desire and intention, and the first step of creating what he wills. If he stays true to his desire and intention through focusing, the desire will become one with his Spirit. In ways unknown, the Spirit will move through him and this desire will become flesh and dwell amongst him.

Notice that there was no flesh or tangibility in the beginning that could have been utilized to manifest the thing God desired. There was no money, superior tools, or better environment; there was only a strong desire. Then, in ways that are unknown to men, this desire became flesh. This very same spirit and its creative power lives within every man, and it seeks to express itself through him in the very same fashion.

A man is a medium through which God seeks to express, explore, and experience Himself. This is the fundamental reason why a man must find the manner through which God can express, explore, and experience himself through him, and as him. It should not be any manner that is perhaps convenient, realistic, or accessible, but one that is truly in alignment with his calling.

It is through the process of being and expressing Who You Really Are that you are able to give, and once you start giving and sharing, you do not have to concern yourself about getting the accessories of life. Once a man's thoughts, words, and deeds are in alignment and in harmony with the kingdom within him, and he is operating with the modes operandi of the creative power of the universe, the world around him will thus grant him sevenfold. For a man does not get what he wants, he gets what he is. So, become who you really are, and leave the rest to your Father, for He knows that you need to be fed, clothed, and sheltered.

That is the greatest secret of all. It rests solely within you to know *why* you would love to be and do the thing that you would love to. Within that knowing rests the spirit and faith that will be with you when you pass through deep waters, leading you along unfamiliar paths and turning the darkness into light before you.

The man who knows what he would love to be, do, and have is always on the alert for new information. He has so positioned himself to recognize all helpful ideas visiting his own mind or coming from the mouth of fellow man, ideas and information that might aid him to move towards that which he would love to be, do or have. He is a self-disciplined man. He does not seek to engage in unnecessary and unproductive activities that do not aid him in moving towards what he wants. He does not spend his few resources and time wastefully but invests them. Time and money are not to be spent, but instead invested.

The adage of 'birds of a feather flock together' is not only true in the world of matter, but it is also utterly true in the world of thought, for everything in our visible world was first imagined before it came into the world of matter. Thoughts are the original staff, and thoughts, also flock with their kind in the world of thought.

The Law of Attraction states *that which is like unto itself is drawn*. This is evident to the mortal eye, and it is for this reason that birds of a feather flock together, and because it is so in the world of matter, one can see why it is essential that a man knows exactly what he would love to be and do. The moment he decides what it is he would love to be and do, he focuses his point of attraction, and by aligning with the Law of Attraction, thoughts, people, circumstances, events, and experiences of a kind (which are birds of a kind) will be attracted by him (thus flocking with him). Opportunities leading towards the fulfilment of that which he would love to be, do, or have will start dropping into his life, and because he knows what he desires, he is better positioned and prepared to harness the thoughts, notice and seize opportunities, and utilize the circumstances that are useful in backing him to achieve his desire.

Where focus goes, energy flows, meaning the thing what you focus on expands. This truth is overwhelmingly demonstrated in the daily life of men. Soccer fanatics are drawn to one another because of this law, the religion fanatics, fashion lovers and business man prefer to hang with their kind, the wine lovers are always on the lookout for their kind to down a glass, because that is where their focus is and they in-turn flock with men who just like themselves. Knowing this, one can shift and direct his attention to the thing he would love to experience, and he is sure to bring it about in his own experience through this law.

A man who does not know what he would love to be and do will waste his time and effort by engaging in all sorts of businesses proposals and business ideas trying to take a bite at success, and will wastefully invest his resources in projects and programs just to later find him in a place of regret.

I know a young man who once came moaning to me in regret, after investing his hard-earned money in a business idea he was not passionate about and had little interest in. He learned later that the project required skills and responsibilities he was unable to contribute, due to his lack of training and education. I blame him not, for he, like a thousand of us in this world, did not know what he wanted to be and do in life. All he wanted at that point in time was to dive into an opportunity that seemed to promise advancement and beauty. There are many of his kind in this world, who spend and invest their resources in the hope to open the door that leads to prosperity, but it often is in vain. The hunger and desperateness to step into the realm of wealth, which is perceived as a place of happiness and freedom, is at the highest the world has ever witnessed. Any man who does not know what he would love to be and do will end up like this young man. For if you do not know what you would love to be and do, all you ever want is to have, to gain, and to gain quickly. In this mindset, you find yourself befriending fear and desperation, and jumping at every idea or project that promises a profit. You either set yourself up to be an easy target, prone to the trap of exploitation set up by those around you, or you become a dangerous creature, harming anyone who seems to be in your way. Fear of failure will soon sneak into your mind, and you will migrate from creative innovation to competitive building, where you will start to attain 'things' at all cost, thus losing your soul in the process.

People around the world are desperately seeking change and a chance for beauty and grace. Glamour has become the new order and the language of the new age, and the sad phenomenon happening around the world with false prophets taking advantage of helpless and hopeless souls is no coincidence. Many a man will approach you in the form of prophets and saviours, promising the desperate souls all the kingdom of the world through cash and status.

Temptation, it seems, comes to us when we are in a place of hardship, during discomfort, inconvenience, and when we are most vulnerable. It comes when everything in the world seems to be going against us. It visits us when we are tied to a narrow sphere of limited finances or confidence, like at the time it came to visit my acquaintance who was desperately waiting on a chance that would give him a ride to an arena of honey and milk.

Be watchful of your fellow man and his intentions as he approaches you. We are told a drama of Jesus being tempted when he was in the wildness for forty days, hungry from eating nothing. He was led to a high place and shown all the kingdoms of the world, and promised to be given all authority over the kingdoms and all their glory. But the Prophet born of Mary was no ordinary man. He knew the truth, and he countered temptation with the truth combined with faith. If we can only know the truth that we will intolerantly lean onto, even when times are hard and pressing, we will have found our true saviour and his kingdom that is within us.

A time ago, in my own experience, I was close to being a victim of a dishonest scheme. Months after graduation, my search for a job had been proven to be in vain. Desperate and seeking change, I ran into an agent on the internet promising me a great opportunity, and chance for beauty and grace was within reach, or so I thought. The opportunity required that I pay a hefty sum of money upfront for the process of my employment to be concluded. Young, inexperienced, and untested in the real world outside of college, I failed to look deeper into the details of the offer that was tabled before me. Admittedly, as it was to Eve in the Garden of Eden, the fruit was pleasant to my eyes, and also desiring independence and freedom, I was a few feet away from picking the fruit to take a bite. Thanks, be to the woman who came from the West, my Mother, who one day after a few document exchanges had transpired between me and the agent, came right into my room one morning while I was still in bed and said, "I have a bad feeling, I hardly slept yesterday night, something is pretty odd about the job offer you are on." I am normally a stubborn creature, especially if I want something, but with a few failed attempts and money wasted prior to this saga, I dared to listen to my Mother on this instance. She left a one hundred dollar note on my counter as she stormed out of my room and immediately left for work. Thanks to her, I was unlike Eve, and did not eat the fruit, though good and pleasant for the eyes. I jumped out of bed immediately, switched on the computer, and went on the internet and pulled up the company profile. There was two different contacts, one for an office situated in the west and another situated in the south eastern part of the world. I dialed the office situated in the west, and a lady picked up the line. Before she could utter a word, I deliberately jumped in and asked if this was perhaps the office in the south east, and behold, she said yes. Immediately I knew my mother was right, and instantly, I also had realized that my communicating with the agent was strictly confined to electronic-mail. Each time I attempted to reach out to him telephonically, he would mostly tell me how busy he is and advising me to e-mail him, claiming it to be a more convenient form of communication. Looking back and connecting the dots, I realized without a shadow of a doubt that it was a scam. Hard earned money was highly at stake and I was a few steps away to being robbed.

I was desperate for change, seeking a chance for beauty and grace, and I did not have a desire in mind for what I was working on. All I wanted was an opportunity that promised prosperity. Then came an agent (with ill intentions), promising me all the kingdoms of the world.

This drama of Jesus, as we are told in the bible, unfolds in our daily lives in innumerable ways. In business dealings, value exchanges, and in relationships (many a time has a man approached a lover who is desperately seeking a chance for affection and love). Without hope, all the kingdoms of the world can be promised and accepted, just to be thrown away a few days later after getting what they actually signed up for, that is, dismay.

Our desire should not be of wanting to attain material wealth, merely because we are trying to portray a picture of success and happiness, for happiness is never deposited in dusty accessories of life. Happiness is found through expressing Who We Really Are, so our motive and intent in life should be to express our true life's calling. Once you know what you would love to be and do in life, you are unlikely to fall into any trap of exploitation. We can guard and protect our desires, and let no man destroy them with dubious intentions.

You should know why you want to be and do what you would love to, and you will need to be projecting a clear desire to the universe, thus softening resistance that might block the manifestation of your desire. Your desire will become definite, subjected to the womb of your spirit. Since spirit seeks to embody the form which we imagine, by law, it must embody the form which you have focused and impressed upon it, and you can be assured that it will.

Know WHY you would love to be, do, and have,
WHAT you would love to be, do, and have, and,
start at once doing the things you would love to do and
the things you would love to have will be given unto you; you
don't have to know HOW.

-Muzire Mbuende - 2016

CHAPTER 4
HOW?

How you will achieve your dream

"You must be the change you wish to see in the world" – Mahatma Gandhi

The question in the mind of every man with a desire is, 'How can I achieve my dream,' The quest for *'how'* one can achieve his dreams is perhaps the major obstacle that has paralyzed many a man across the face of the earth. Not because there are indeed no clear steps on how to achieve the dream, but because it is the wrong type of approach to begin with. We must keep in mind that it is our intention that encourages the means to show up. That is the Law. For, just as the means of expression of a seed lies within the seed itself, so does the plans of self-expression of our desires lie within the desire itself.

I would encourage you to read the above sentence again. Just to make sure we drive it home.

From here onwards, this truth should encourage us to divorce the unfortunate notion that we must first have all the instructions or the know-*'how'* to achieve our dreams at our disposal before we can get up and pursue our dreams. Cherishing such a concept is entertaining that ancient adage of putting the cart before the horse and expecting to march forward – it is in essence to work against the law and order of life rather than with it.

If we would have all the resources we need before we start our creative work, then we could rid of faith as a life principle, because then we would be able to become, do, and have anything we want in life, without much struggle. However, this would totally contradict scripture or even the very nature of Spirit. For thoughts precede matter, and not the other way around; Thought as a genesis of creation needs the backing of faith for it to manifest in its physical equivalent. Because faith, in essence, we are told is *'the substance'* of the thing we hope for. We cannot have the thing we hope for without first holding its substance – faith. Scripture does not tell us that the availability of instructions and resources at our disposal is the substance of the things we hope for, but faith. So, we cannot now thwart the law of Nature and Spirit through which things are made and attempt to employ our own understanding and laws, but if we are to succeed in realizing our desires than we are only to employ the laws and follow the modus operandi of Spirit.

Desires are the cause of everything that is and that will ever be. Therefore, desire yields the plans, so the '*how*' or the means of realization of a dream sleeps within the dream itself.

A desire is a formless substance formed in the world of thought, or dare I say, in heaven. Now one cannot think or have a desire without the use of words, for words are the cloth of thoughts. I can, without hesitation, prove the above statement, for it is recorded in scripture, where it states that, "In the beginning was the *Word* and the *Word* was with God, and the *Word* was God." and then, "The *Word* became flesh and made his dwelling among us…"

Thus, it is the *Word* (or the desire, or the thing that we would love to be, do, or have) that is first conceived, and then upon being focused it becomes a conviction and thus we begin through inspired action to clothe the thing we desire.

So, the genesis in the process of creation is the *Word*, the thought, the desire and not the resources or information. Our desire must be the focal point, and then as we keep this desire in our minds eye and taking deliberate action towards the attainment of our desire, the resources and instruction we need will be provided.

Reality is not the seedling of dreams, but the other way around. James Allen knew this when he said, "Dreams are the seedlings of reality,". Dreams are not children of reality, but it is reality that is the child of dreams. So, we do not depend on the resources that are on the external, but on the invisible and infinite resources within us to make real our dreams.

Return To Your Imagination

"When we use our imagination properly it is our greatest friend; it goes beyond reason and is the only light that takes us everywhere." – Swami Vivekanda

Necessity might be the mother of invention, but to invent something new or to better an existing product or device, it is to one apparatus that a man must and can return: our own wonderful human imagination. But we are also told that, "Through him all things were made; without him nothing was made that has been made".

Now the question arises, who is 'him' referred to in the scriptures, through which things were made, and that without 'him' nothing was made that has been made? While in the land of the individual, we all are aware of the eternal truth that there is not a man-made thing that came into being without first having been *imagined.*

Is it not out of the imaginative mind of man that the aeroplane, automobile, television, radio, computer, chair, and everything else that exists in the world of the individual came into being for convenience of man and the advancement of life? Writers, musician, painters, and all artists know this to be the only one gateway that leads to the manifestation of their art. It is the only faculty that enables a man to see and interpret that which the world and fellow man cannot. Imagination I believe is short for:

image-nation, which means the mind is a nation that consist of spiritual images, sleeping dormant in the womb of the mind and through focusing (by using the vehicle of thought) on these images, which are just mere possibilities – a man can select his ideal image, a spiritual prototype and download and transport it from the nation of formless images into the nation of form.

So, who is this agent through which all things came into existence if it is not our own wonderful human imagination from which the spring of life flows? What could it be that John was referring to that is the source of all that has been made? While to our knowledge only imagination has demonstrated itself to be the only one agent that is able to stretch its hand into the deep, dark, and void, and catch imagined unseen-formless-things and possibilities and make them appear in the land of the individual. Surely it cannot be a man of flesh and blood, for only *human imagination* has given birth to all man-made things. It cannot be a man of flesh that was born of Mary, for we are told that, "'He' was with God in the beginning". Now who is 'He' that was in the beginning with God?

Is 'He' not the 'Word' that was in the beginning with God? For we are also told, "In the beginning was the Word, and the Word was with God, and the Word was God".

Is this not *imagination*? the faculty that carries Words? The abode that houses words as thought-pictures or in the form of images? So, the 'He' referred in the scriptures is nothing else but our own wonderful human *imagination*. Through imagination, everything is, that has been made, and without imagination no-thing has and can be made.

So now that a vision of the work you are called to do is occasionally being flashed across your conscious mind as you go about your life affairs, trusting and determined to materialize it, it is to your own wonderful human imagination you must return; for it is the only agent through which your vision can come to fruition.

By impressing your vision upon the subconscious mind – the female part of your mind – and by constantly focusing on your vision, and most importantly doing what you can with what you have, you can surely move towards the attainment of your dream.

Impressing our desire upon the subconscious mind is to allow conception, and once conception has taken place in the invisible womb that is our subconscious mind, we must be like a faithful gardener and nurture our seed. By ways only known to herself with time, our subconscious mind (the mother of creation) will project in our environment the vision we have impressed upon it.

But it is paramount in our creative process, that we move and '*do*' the work. For Spirit can only do what Spirit can do, and that is to guide, to give a hint, communicate to us through intuition, through a feeling, a surge; prompting us to do something that will move us closer to our desire. Therefore, the body as a vehicle through which the Spirit seeks to express Itself must move and do the work required to be done in order that we may attain our desire.

Our own wonderful human imagination is the only agent to which we must return, fully trusting that it will show us the way we are to undertake in order to give birth to the child that is our vision. This truth sleeps in the words of Joseph Murphy, when he said, "When the world says, 'It is impossible, it can't be done', the man with a disciplined, controlled and directed imagination says, "It is done!"

But I would like to add to his beautiful line and say, "The man with a disciplined, controlled, and directed imagination, coupled with action and faith says, "It is done!", for it is a walk of faith.

It Is a Walk of Faith

The educational system together with the corporate world promises to provide certainty and security in the future for the man who remains disciplined and toes its conventional line. The education system teaches a man to do certain things in a certain way and shows him '*how*' a thing can be achieved, and if he commits and carries these instructions out to the letter, he is sure to progress further up the grades until he finally graduates.

Now while this approach is sound and relevant in the educational and corporate world, and one can achieve great things in that line of work, it has rather a negative impact on the nature of men. For it does not nurture and grow his *intuition*, his God given guiding-system, the most important tool that he will need in creating and achieving his hearts desires. The educational system unconsciously programs him to ignore and forget his inner guiding system and encourages him to solely depend on his rational mind and external assistance in the endeavoring to complete his projects, his assignments and eventually his certificates.

Now so many graduates come out into the world wanting to follow and live out their visions and dreams and seek to apply the same approach which they have been taught behind the school fences; of relying on their rational mind, being logical and practical, the concept of first figuring out the '*how*', or having all the information and resources at their disposal before they can assemble their projects, before they can get off their butts and take massive action towards the attainment of their goals. And the moment they cannot seem to figure out the '*how*', fear creeps in, and the project is immediately set aside for a tomorrow that never comes, and many a times abandoned for good; for they have not been taught and are unaware that they can depend on another powerful tool, a tool within themselves that can assist them in completing their projects, their hearts desires, besides the conventional approach of relying on their rational mind or external resources. And so, they remain stagnant and feel stuck.

You might not want to believe this, but do you think it quite a coincidence that the most successful people by far that, the world has ever known are mostly college dropouts or individuals with no formal education whatsoever? Why? Because these individuals have escaped your conventional programming on how projects are completed, the educational training on how to achieve things; they have on their own, in their own ways, through trial and error, through mentors, and other schools of thought learned to follow their hearts; they have learned to listen to their intuitive whispers, to rely-on and to trust the Inner-Divine Guidance rather than outer cacophony, practicality or the lines and rules set out by others. They have come to grasp that the information and the resources they need lies within their desires. These are the people who knows and understands that security, certainty, fulfillment, and true freedom are found within and not without.

Now, I am not putting this out to merely highlight the weakness of the educational system, or to discredit its conventional approach. I believe that education is great a weapon any human can and should equip themselves with. But it is my firm intent to bring an awareness which will encourage men the word over to realize that, to live out one's vision, to realize his dream, one needs to go deeper within himself, that he must lean in and listen to his intuition, to tell him that he must rely on that germ of intelligence that sleeps within him, his Inner Power, to tell him that all he ever needed to make his dreams come true lies within himself, that he may fearlessly embark upon the journey to make his dreams come true. For it is a walk of faith and not of logic.

It is apparent that engineers, architects, lawyers, and doctors are noble professions and necessary to sustain and advance life, and there are those who are called into this lines of work; it is admirable to stay on a path of certainty and security if you think that it is your space to occupy in life, but if your soul is completely on a different track than that which you are being and doing right now, if you long for more and believe within your soul that there is more for you, believe me - there is.

Industrial machines, computers, and automobiles are daily improved and made anew, faster and more convenient than ever before because of a touch of some level of education. So, education is a necessary weapon that rightfully occupies its space in the world, and its effect can be witnessed the world over. The world is advancing and growing anew in leaps and bounds. But unlike the educational system that has a laid-out blueprint and a clear path to follow or a 9am - 5pm grind that requires a certain training, punctuality and some level of loyalty - the path to live out your vision calls for faith more than it does, rationality. Creativity requires of a man to utilize his imagination. It demands of him to be resolute and determined in the picture he sees within his soul, to have faith in it, even if fellow men, or the world at large, are enabled to comprehend his ways - to trust that the *'how'* that bears the tools and the resources he will need to make real his vision, will be revealed to him as he walks the path towards the attainment of his desire.

The route to the corporate world has been systematically normalized by the government, and men and women all over the worlds are now compelled to toe this traditional line; go to school, get to a college, get a job, pay taxes, buy a house, pay the bills, take care of the debts, retire and wait to check the heck out. For who? For the financial and time freedom of those in power. They encourage men and women to be practical and responsible, to be good and law-abiding citizens, to toe the established lines; convincing the masses that in the absence of a college degree, you are bound to become a nobody in life. An utter myth, and it should not be true for any human being. They have deliberately reversed the law and the paradigm of life as taught in the scriptures, that says, 'First seek ye the kingdom of God, and these things shall be added unto you.' They are instructing men to be responsible, work hard and to add *'all these things first'*, (the accessories and toys of life), and retire and, hopefully, if everything works out fine, the *kingdom of God* (your desires, time freedom, fulfilment and abundance) shall be added unto you later in life.

And also, the government together with the private sector systems have been deliberately designed to compensate a man just enough to sustain him, to make sure he just gets by, just enough to where he is afraid and enable to not quit his job, just enough to where he is forced to work hard that he may keep his job, for another Joe is waiting in line and ready to take over. So, the idea of working hard to first add *'these things'* (the material things of life) and then seeking the *'kingdom of God'* thereafter is a wrongdoing, for soon a man realizes that he has endowed himself with so much responsibility (mortgage, debt, bills, car allowance, small ones to take care of) that it becomes almost impossible for him to quit his job and get out of the corporate system to pursue his dreams, and in that, he is trapped for life to the degree that he sees this way of being a normal way of life, for almost everyone is doing the same thing. Well it is not, for it is a system that has deliberately been orchestrated by people just like him so they can have their freedom on top of his back.

We go through life substituting the principles and laws of life with our own rational mind, complemented and justified by the rules and lines set by others, being practical, rational, and responsible as we are told, just to find ourselves feeling empty and dissatisfied, full of anxiety and fear, longing for more and looking for answers in the wrong places. Yet, the answers have been sleeping in the scriptures for eons where we have been encouraged, "… not be worried about your life, as to what you will eat or what you will drink; nor for your body, as to what you will put on. Is not life more than food, and the body more than clothing?"

We must not at all concern ourselves with the attainment of the accessories of life but through our very being and doing strive to choose life; to advance and better it through the light we decide to shine. We must choose the path of living out our vision. Through this righteous and noble act, all the things we want will be added unto us. We must fearlessly choose the narrow path.

"...For wide is the gate and broad is the way that leads to destruction, and many enter through it. But small is the gate and narrow the road that leads to life, and only a few find it." The courageous few.

The broad path in life leads to modern day slavery and mediocrity, as it has tied many great men to the 9-5 dead-end humdrum routine, doing what they don't want to do, underselling themselves, leaving them unfulfilled and hoping and yearning for more, whereas the narrow path leads a man to a path of freedom, fulfillment and abundance, and the courageous few travel it. You cannot stay on the broad path travelled by many and yet yearn for the narrow path results. It is only through the expression of your light - by being thyself - the path of living out your calling, that you can taste the results of the narrow path.

Among the emotions of the mind, nothing has a cutting-edge force like the emotion of faith, through which, if harnessed and cherished, one can surely move mountains. Faith is your wand; this we are informed through the biblical drama of Moses and The Water of Meribah.

Now, in this drama, the rock holds an invisible resource that lies dormant but within reach, and the rod represents an act of trust and faith. Unlike Moses, who did not believe in the whisper of The Voice of Truth within him, we must believe and trust in our inner whisper and adhere to the instructions given to us and go forward and strike the rock (this means realizing the dormant resources and making use of them), which will gush out the means that will help us get rid of our seemingly current difficulties and put us on a forward trajectory towards the attainment of our vision.

This is not a mere theory to utter, but an eternal truth. The most creative people in the world, who changed the trajectory of life, who against all odds stood firm even when subjected to the most brutal suffering and pain in an attempt to get them to give up their pursuits, who at times and at all cost were ready to trade their life at the hands of those who dared to stand in their ways, these brilliants people leaned unto nothing else but a sheer emotion of faith in their vision and in what they wanted to see manifest.

These are the individuals who dared to listen to the inner-silent voice in their soul rather than to the external pessimistic and threatening forces, and, through their persistence, their visions were proven to be sound and eventually became a reality.

To have faith is to strongly believe and know that the thing we desire has already come to pass, to know that our prayer has been answered, to hold onto the spiritual prototype of the thing we wish to make manifest, to feel it to be true and real, to know that you have conceived, and to be a faithful mother and bear the child that is your desire gracefully.

The one born in the Transkei was a faithful conceiver. He believed in and pursued the ideal of a democratic and free society in which all persons could live together in harmony, peace, and equal opportunities for all, an ideal which he fearlessly pursued to achieve, but also, if need be, an ideal he was prepared to die for. Such was Nelson Mandela's conviction of his vision even when he was locked behind bars for 27 years on an isolated (Robben) Island.

The apartheid regime was desperate to hang on to power, ergo did everything in the book to demoralize the mental-spirit of Madiba and other black liberation strugglers in prison and those outside who cherished the idea of equality and freedom for all South Africans. Now, the idea of throwing in the towel would have been a rational act and, an idea I believe visited Madiba's mind often, especially given the fact that he was sentenced to life imprisonment. But one day, looking out his tiny window, a thought dawned on him that, 'What if this is perhaps part of the process that would enable my people to be freed'? And with the last strength he could muster, he hung onto this single idea that seemed to be the only line that carried with it a silver lining of hope, that his ideal was perhaps possible. South Africa is far from becoming a rainbow nation and an equal society as he hoped for, but in 1994, Nelson Mandela went on to become the first black president of the very country that was presided by those who had imprisoned him before he was released in 1991.

It is often wise and rational to listen to advice from fellow men, and they might have concrete evidence in the world to back their advice, but the ultimate favor we can do to ourselves is to catch and honor the vision that God has entrusted us with and trust in it more than anything from the external.

"…seek first His kingdom'…, 'and all these things will be added to you."

For as you first seek the 'kingdom' (your vision), everything, all the help, all the tools, 'all these things' that you need to make real your vision, 'will be added unto you'.

"Ask, and it will be given to you; seek, and you will find; knock, and it will be opened to you".

As you constantly ask, the answers and ways to your vision will be given to you; as you seek, you shall find all the resources you need to make real your vision; as you knock, the doors that will advance you to attain your vision will be opened unto you.

Just as children stumbles, falls, and persistently gets back up in their pursuit to walk, they are surely soon to figure out their balance with both their feet and eventually begin to walk. In the same way, you must trust the process in the pursuit of making real your vision, for there is no other path except the very process (of falling and getting back up) a child undergoes in their pursuit to walk.

But you must have faith in Yourself, faith in a mighty power so near, ever-ready, and excited to flow through you - to express itself through you.

No man has ever achieved anything great, without believing they will. Have faith in that something that whispers from within, the same faith that has been demonstrated by every great character in history: Alexander the Great, Henry Ford, Guglielmo Marconi, Alexander Graham Bell, and Oprah Winfrey. For only those who believe in their ideas and visions, and act on them, bring them to fruition. Every religion, every community forward movement, and every creed must have its beginning and existence based on faith by the one who initiated it before it ever touched the surface of the earth.

We must have assurance in our ideal, in our vision that resides in our souls. We must be sure of it, sure about it, not because we can touch and see it with our senses, but because we can feel it within our heart of hearts. We must continue to see what we want, and only that, to assume and affirm what we desire as real, because we have been taught to say '*I am*', '*I have*', *it is mine*', *we must claim it,*' even in the absence of evidence. "Let the weak man say, 'I am strong'," and let him who 'has-not' say 'I have'.

There is a constant hollering in the Bible along the lines of '*your faith*', "Your faith has healed you", "Their faith has healed you," and "O ye of little faith!"

And one may wonder why so much emphasis and substance has been invested in faith in scripture. It is all because dreams and visions are not rational and practical, but rather, by their nature - are spiritual, and to make them real, faith is required. Faith is to spirit what fuel is to an automobile; if directed towards the attainment of something, that something is sure to be realized. Of all explanations of faith found in all the good books on planet earth, nothing defines it as utterly beautiful as the definition found in scripture, "Faith is being sure of what we hope for, being convinced of what we do not see".

Throughout the Bible, faith is the command we find greatly emphasized, for the book deals with the science of the mind of the individual and seeks to whisper to men how to release his own soul from the bondage of Pharaoh and the walls of the Jericho of his own making.

"God said, 'Let there be light,' and there was light." One might be tempted to ask, How? Out of pure desire, the Father arose into consciousness and allowed light to be, out of the essence of the Spirit itself. "Allow," He said, not "*how* can I make light?" or, "From what can I make light? since I have no resources" He simply said allow that which already is to be transformed from the seemingly formless, void, and dark substance into light; for science tell us that, "Energy cannot be created or destroyed, but can only be transformed from one form to another. The Father did not have external means readily available before Him. There were no resources from which he had to create the light. For scripture tells us that the earth was formless, void, and dark. Not from outside, but from within, he called the light into being. Remember, we are created in the image and the likeness of the Father, so in truth, within us sleeps the ability to call forth our light - our desires into being, by simply desiring and commanding it. Desire is the vehicle that reveals the method of attainment - it yields the means and plans. We should always remember the eternal truth that God cannot implant in us a desire without also giving us the ability and opportunities to help us actualize our desire. Just as in the process of problem solving in mathematics, in manipulation, solving for 'x', where the solution to solving 'x' is normally contained within the problem to be solved itself, so do desires and dreams contain within themselves the plans of self-expression.

"The oak sleeps in the acorn; the bird waits in the egg; and in the highest vision of the soul a waking angel stirs. Dreams are the seedlings of realities", wrote James Allen. With the aid of the nutrients from the soil and the energy from the sun; the expressed trunk, branches, and the leaves of the oak tree sleep within the acorn. The expressed flesh, veins, tendon, blood, bones, and feather of a bird waits in the egg. So also do the plans of self-expression lie within the seed of your desire.

'But!' is perhaps one of the greatest excuses that has crippled men and women in all the corners of the world. People of all races and religions have developed an unfortunate habit of identifying all the excuses of why they cannot achieve their desires, or of how their dreams will never come to pass. We have been so programmed with this wrong pattern of thinking that we end up believing and concluding that there are no ways in this infinite world of infinite ways that we can utilize to achieve our hearts desires, just because we cannot see them.

The word, '*but!*' is one of the greatest shackles that bind the majority of men across the face of the earth, and in truth, these shackles are not external, but are internal shackles that bind the feet and wrists of their own imaginations and beliefs. If a man truly awakens, he will realize that the excuse 'but!' has proved itself abundantly to him that it does not aid him at all, but rather sends him further down and deeper into an arena of failure. So, it is paramount to notice this and begin telling a different story. A positive story, a story of courage, faith and optimism, a resourceful story like "I can, and I will do it," or "I am sure to find a way to realize my dream", which will in turn change his attitude and habits, a new way of doing things and surely his future for the better.

Words are nothing by themselves, as words are merely labels, or symbols, that are useful to help describe things. They are not the experience itself. The experience which they represent or attempt to convey is not contained within them. That which they convey is invisible, and it is the invisible that should be employed by the man. Words have only the reality of ink and paper, so by telling himself a certain word or story, he can employ (or not employ) the invisible instructions. The invisible message represented by the words could be an instruction for him to act or to be idle. So, by knowing this, he has the power within him to instruct himself positively by telling himself a word or a story that will prompt him to act or a message that will condemn him to idleness.

Knowing this, I urge you to tell yourself a message that will prompt you to do something propelling you in the direction of achieving your dream.

The how is not yours to be concerned about. In truth, it is beyond the comprehension of man to discover, for it operates within the spiritual realm. It is only the Life-Force within us that sees all, hears all, and that has the power and knowledge through the Law of Attraction to orchestrate and arrange all the details to harmoniously bring forth our desire.

As a gardener plants his seed in the womb of creation with absolute faith that it will grow and bear fruit, so should you turn your desire over to the infinite intelligence within you, acknowledging in your heart that it has the answer and the "know how" of accomplishment. Look at the magic and miracle-power in the life of a seed. No matter the way in which a gardener buries the seed in the earth, even without aid in the darkness of the soil it does not grow chaotically, for within the seed is an intelligence that knows and senses the direction of the gravitational field, thus orientating the roots to grow deeper into the earth, attracting to it only the ingredients that help the plant grow. Likewise, the shoots on top (stalk and leaves) are attracted towards the light, as the leaves only seek the light source that help the plant grow.

The roots of a plant know they have to remain in the ground, because that is where their livingness is, and the shoots on top part that bear leaves and fruits seeks the light for its livingness is in the outer space. Such power and wisdom is bestowed in a tiny little seed which we deem it has little conscious compared to us. Yet the miracle demonstrated by such a tiny thing is so profound and such a great message. If we can invest the same faith in our dream, our desire will in like manner be attracting only its affinities and the sources that will help it manifest into the material world. Once we focus and impress it upon our mind, it will in like manner only seek and be attracted by the events, ideas, circumstances and people that will aid it to grow and bear the fruit we seek.

We chew and swallow food, without worrying about how the food will be distributed in our body. Look at the magic of the Intelligent-Power that administers and satisfies every cell and fibre, every bone and hair, as well lubricating every joint without our consent and making sure every toe and finger on our body is not starved to decay. There is an intelligence within us that, we cannot put a finger on it, but I know it is- for all I know.

We must be watchful, for as soon as we set an intention, seemingly small circumstances will begin to show themselves. Though small, we have to treat them with professionalism and do what is required at that point in time. A small doing of this circumstance will lead to another seemingly small event, and so on, until we are guided to the attainment of the thing that we would love to be, do, or have. It is only after having that which we initially sought to be, do, or have, that looking back, we will be able to connect the dots of how every seemingly small circumstance was crucial in guiding and pushing us in the right direction. It is the opportunity, information, or direction that these minor events push us to that are vital and should be considered, and not the magnitude of the circumstances.

"…Not by might nor by power, but by My Spirit," were the words of the Lord to Zerubbabel. Ask, become, and immediately start doing whatever small deed you can do with what you have and where you are, and you will then be catered to with more data as you go along.

We are told His ways are past finding out, for scripture beckons to us, "Can you discover the depths of God? Can you discover the limits of the Almighty? No man of flesh and blood can fathom the ways of God.

Look to the mysterious drama of the birth of the Christ. This message testifies that every living soul is highly favored by God, because occasionally every living soul has the angel Gabriel visit him. The angel Gabriel represents a good idea, an inspiration, or a desire about a possible business venture, or an idea for an invention, that would drop and float in our minds out of the blue in our dreams or during the day as we go about our daily affairs. In this drama, Jesus represents the nature of your desire, or the thing that you would love to be, do, or have, and once accepted, it will be able to manifest. Mary represents you, and every time an inspiration, idea, or desire drops into your mind, you, as Mary, ask the question, 'but *how*?' "How can this be, since I am a virgin?"

In the life of the individual this question comes in the form of, "*How* can I achieve my dream while circumstances do not allow me?" "*How* can that be, when I have no formal education or college degree?" "*How* can I have or do that when I have little or no money"? "*How* can I be that, when the environment and conditions are discouraging"? "*How* can I actualize my hearts desires, when I have no connections or network"?

The message we all ought to project our attention to in these dramas is the truth that, *'Nothing is impossible with God.'* This was not a braggadocios statement. These words came to pass and Mary gave birth to a character called Jesus Christ, your savior and your desire. The God to whom 'nothing is impossible' is not a God sited somewhere out of reach of our being and existence, such as the God that religion teachers and students have fashioned. God lives in us, as us. He is the very Spirit of our being, the very current of life flowing through us and breathing us, seeking to reveal It-self through us, as a beautifully created vessel, through which He can express and experience Himself. For as Alfred Tennyson said, "closer is He than breathing, and nearer than hands and feet."

The Wright brothers dreamed of a machine that would travel and transport man through the ether, like the birds of the sky. They had no formal education. Their father was a devoted priest and told them to abandon their idea, for it would land them in hell. But like Mary, they embraced the idea and walked persistently over contempt, fear, and limitation as if walking on unmarked graves, and today evidence of their faith and their sound dream can be witnessed the world over.

The only attitude and response required from us is to accept and embrace the idea that has been tossed into our mind as Mary did. We must express our agreement to the idea, just as we would listen to the angel Gabriel, and say, "May it happen to me according to your word," in which case the process, or the *how*, will commence to assemble and actualize our desire. Blessed is he who believes that the Lord's word to him will be fulfilled."

Know now that nothing is impossible to Him who lives in you and you in Him, and that the thing that you would love to be, do, or have will actualize just like the mysterious birth of the Christ, if you accept and believe in your desire.

In a like manner to the womb of a woman which can actualize the embryo that has been conceived, so can the mind achieve whatever it has conceived. "There is nothing you can dream that the mind you thought it up in doesn't know how to achieve."

Ask, and immediately migrate to being and doing what you would love to be and do. Start doing what you can do, where you are, with what you have, and do not ask *how* the big picture of the puzzle will come together. Whether you start right in the middle, the bottom, or the top of a puzzle, it is sure to be completed, and your desire will come together, if you just dare to start. Walk in faith that it is already given to you, and soon, in a time not known to you, that which you would love to have will externalize. Walk in faith, and emphasize action, as you should *do* what you can, where you are, with what you have; do! Do, because scripture tells us that, "faith by itself, if it is not complemented by action, is dead."

Walk in faith for, "faith is the substance of things hoped for, the evidence of things not seen". It is the substance, meaning it is the garment with which we clothe, the thing we want to take out of the void and dark and enable it to see and feel the light of day.

The mere fact that we cannot see or do not know the ways of how our dreams will come to pass is not proof that there are no ways or plans. "Absence of evidence is not evidence of absence." We should come to realize this truth now, and our faith should rest in the knowledge that we have eyes that are limited; they can only see around us to a certain extent. We have ears, but finite they are; they can only hear from a measurable distance, and only through specific ranges. Solely because of that, engrave in your heart faith in the wisdom of Him who knows all, hears all, and sees all. He surely has in His toolbox all the tools and knowledge that will assist you in accomplishing that which you would love to be, do, or have.

Live, walk, and breathe in the truth that we do not live outside of that which is called God, and we do not move outside of that which is termed as God. We do not breathe outside of that which is labeled God, nor do we clothe, eat, drink, or sleep outside of that which is called God. The abode of God called heaven is not a place situated in a location outside of us, and far from our being and existence, but "…in Him we live and move and have our being." In Him, not outside of Him; not far from Him, but in Him. We are living and swimming in a pool called God.

Every single man and woman, hundreds of thousands they may be, that will assist us in attaining our desire, are but servants purposely and harmoniously lined up by that which is God. All the circumstances that will assist us in our journey as we march towards the attainment of the thing that we would love to be, do, or have are arranged by the invisible and infinite intelligence called God. For the Lord Almighty says, "Not by might nor by power, but by my Spirit." Him, and only Him, rightfully places the components suitable to assist us in attaining the thing that we would love to be, do or have, and thus give birth to the light we wish to emit on earth. Therefore, the how should be our least concern.

God lives in you, using you as his vessel, through which He seeks to reveal Himself. The formless God created form through which He can express, explore, and experience Himself as what he knows Himself to be. This is the greatest secret that only sublime minds have come to know, and now it is given to you to also know this truth.

Believe that a formless and infinite God lives in you, and because He is formless and infinite, He knows no time and space as your finite body and logic has come to know. This is fundamentally why the *'how'* you wish to know is beyond your ken to discover. Your power is not contained within your limited body, but it is your body that is contained within your limitless power.

The greatest analogy that can be used in comparison to the ways of God is the Global Positioning System (GPS). If we can invest the very same faith in God that we have invested in the GPS, we will come to realize at last that we on our own have complicated things that are in truth uncomplicated. We can now realize that we owe it to ourselves to have even more faith in the Architect of the Universe, compared to the trust we have invested in a GPS device created by men of flesh and blood. When a man inserts the destination, he wishes to reach into the GPS, he does not for a minute concern himself as to *how* the GPS will land him at his destination. He may encounter a few delays and face obstacles along the way, but no matter the challenges he faces along the way, if he but faces in the direction of his destination and keeps moving towards it, he will ultimately reach his goal. Similarly, if a man can pinpoint in his own mind the thing he would love to be, do, or have, and then do what he can with what he has and from where he is, moving in the direction towards his vision, he too is sure to attain his desire. By his rectitude of applying this tested and proven method, he is guaranteed to achieve his dream.

It is through the act of relentlessly doing what you can with what you have, right where you are, and focusing on your dream, and by listening to your intuition as the voice of your operator, that you will set yourself afoot towards the attainment of your dream. This is the only proven creative method that will advance you in the direction of your desire, and better tools will be thrown at you as you go along, to assist and propel you towards the attainment of your desire.

A man can go into a quiet place and shut the door behind him, pray his heart out, or he can engage in visualization and meditation techniques all day long. These activities can only help him so much. Scripture tells us that faith not complimented by action is dead. There is no guru of absolute faith that will tell you that he prayed so hard that he left God with no option but that he throws a bag of money through his roof top. So, it is imperative that we should take decisive action towards the attainment of our dreams. Otherwise we will pray to and believe in a seemingly deaf and non-existing God.

If we are to expand on this thought, let us consider the behavior of a mustard seed. A mustard seed does not denounce and lament about the weight of the soil and the darkness that inundate it once it has been deposited in the earth. But with patience, it roots itself firmly, preparing for the wildest weathers (flood and heavy winds) of adversity, and with faith it cracks and pushes through the soil above it, for it knows and believes, for all I know that, there is light at the end of the tunnel. It pushes through, for that which is within it is far greater than any obstacle that is on its way. It pushes through not only to experience the light, but also to grow and express itself more fully and to feed other living organisms. It is striking, then, that Jesus told us that, "If you have but the faith of a mustard seed, you shall move mountains".

The Walls of Jericho of Your Own Making

The world over, in his heart of hearts, every man yearns to be and do what he is called to do. He wants to enter his city, his land flowing with honey and milk, a city that contains all that his heart desires; his freedom, fulfillment, abundance and peace. Yet this city seems to be behind a wall, but a wall it is - of his own creation. He is trapped behind a wall he has erected himself. This wall is not an external wall; it is an internal one, all in his own mind. He is often encountering unwanted events, and he is quick to label them accidents and happenstance and tying their origin to external forces wanting to rob him of progress and success, not knowing it is his own thoughts that have the power of life and the power of death, the power of ill and the power of joy, the power of impotence and the power of freedom, of limitation and so the power of liberation.

Some men I observe hold an intolerant and misleading view that, they are inherently holy and that nothing could possibly be wrong with them. This believe, has let them to blame their shortcomings in life on everything else but themselves, has let them to blame their environment. He is quick to blame his background, his circumstances, the government, or his parents. Even the religious fanatics are still blaming Adam and Eve for their own wrongdoing and sins to this day. "He is born of sin", he claims. He does this without knowing that, he has been a subject of his own environment, he has been programmed by his parents, teachers, and friends to think, perceive and act in a certain way since his childhood. This programming (fake ideas and limiting beliefs from fellow men) has become the very bricks that he has used to erect the walls of his own prison. Only the few who have stopped in their tracks to know themselves, to examine themselves and their own thoughts, perceptions, habits and attitude have come to realize that, the battle of life takes place within the mind and not outside. Because of this awareness, they are able to identify the root symptom, and thusly walk out from the prison of their own creation that has been ajar all along. James Allen knew that the bondage and limitation of man is not on the outside, but within when he said that,

"Mind is the Master power that moulds and makes,
And Man is Mind, and evermore he takes the tool of thought,
and, shaping what he wills,
brings forth a thousand joys, a thousand ills:
He thinks in secret, and it comes to pass:
Environment is but his looking-glass."

By taking the tool of thought and using it for idle-thinking, blaming, and dwelling in the past, man is unconsciously erecting prison walls and locking himself up, and his environment can only mirror his thoughts. For, as within, so without.

Thoughts are the only activity of the mind. This activity, 'thoughts' and inner talks, calls forth our reality. It is because of our own ignorance to this truth that men are unconsciously calling forth unwanted events into their experience. We can argue, deny, and ignore this eternal truth, as many a man has done, but it is not surprising, for we are told that, "He was in the world, and though the world was made through Him, the world did not recognize Him". John 1:10. 'He' is our own wonderful human imagination – our own wonderful thoughts.

"Death and life are in the power of the tongue." said Jesus. We have already established that the tongue can only express the thoughts and images held in our minds in the form of words. So, in essence, death and life lie in the power of the thoughts we choose to entertained in our minds. If this is true without variation than freedom and imprisonment also lies in our minds, and so does plenty and lack, also in bed in our minds. Our tongues and deeds express our highest and focused thoughts, as they are the highest and first command, the genesis of All That Is, the original substances. For," In the beginning was/is the word".

Your thoughts are your wand, and like Moses, with them, the *rock* (your dream) you must strike, which will in turn gush out *water* (your freedom, fulfillment and all your heart's desires), from which humanity will quench their thirst.

As the, "...rain and the snow comes down from heaven, and do not return there without watering the earth. And making it bear and sprout, and furnishing seed to the sower and bread to the eater: So, will My *word* be which goes forth from My mouth; It will not return to Me empty, without accomplishing what I desire, and without succeeding in the matter for which I sent it..." Isaiah 55:10

We have to be careful of the thoughts and images we entertain in our minds, our thoughts, our inner talks, the words we utter to ourselves in silence, for they will not return unto us empty without accomplishing that which we desire and without succeeding in bringing about the physical substance of the thing for which we have sent them. If the words you say are of a limiting nature and fear-based, you are busy erecting walls - behind which only you will be trapped. But if they are positive words, courageous and of determination, resolute and of strong character, inner-talks of faith; the prison walls of your own making will crumble down to dust, and you are sure to go up and possess your city, a city which contain all your hearts desires, a land flowing with honey and milk, the glory of all lands - sure.

The Red Sea of Fear

Men the world over are yearning for freedom, fulfilment and success. However, there seems to be something holding them back, something that is forever pushing the goal post of happiness further away from them, keeping them stagnant and hopeless. It is nothing else but that old enemy of the human race - fear. The one enemy that has robed many a man of their birthright riches since the beginning of time. The fear of looking bad; the fear of putting yourself out there and being vulnerable and up for scrutiny and judgement. The fear of failure, the fear of rejection and being misunderstood, the fear of being perceived as being different and weird from those around us; the fear of not being accepted and loved enough by those around us. That slick and cunning voice, "What if my ideas do not work out"? "What if I fail in my attempts"? "How embarrassing the effort"? These are all but self-limiting internal fears, and they are not real and have no life of their own except the one we give them. They have no life of their own except being given birth and continually being fed, seemingly kept alive and supported by our own consciousness. Fear is not real. It is not founded in a substance-something on the screen of time and space that one can put a finger on. Of course, there is practical fear, such as seeing a lion and fleeing, but the theoretical and emotional fear that we entertain in our minds as we attempt to pursue our dreams is just a natural resisting state of consciousness that arises when you are seeking to grow, seeking to expand, and going after something that is outside of your comfort zone. You will feel it if you dare to step out of the boat, for it will arise like the boisterous winds as we are taught in the great drama of Peter and Jesus at the lake of Galilea. Now many a man goes to church and are often told this great drama and takes it literal and as history fact, yet every living soul must face this boisterous wind if he ever dares to pursue his dream.

Every man has a red sea to cross, something huge and freighting, a thing uncommon and seemingly unlikely that he must overcome. Even the most renowned and idolized individuals who in the eye of many have arrived, had to cross red sea. This red sea arises in the mind, it is psychological, again, that old enemy - fear. It appears in the form of; fear of public speaking, stage fright, wanting to write a book but questioning your writing skills, telling yourself that no one would be interested to hear your story, a business venture you want to start yet questioning your ability and your financial muscle, questioning your background and color. This is all giving into an unreal fear, a red sea within your own mind, formed by thy self - a mere thought you happen to entertain.

You are the Moses, and with your eye fixed on your vision - the land of honey and milk, fear will arise. It will arise in the form of noise in your own mind, bombarding you with questions like the children of Israel, 'Why are you stretching?', 'Who will even bother listening to you', 'Why are you expanding and wanting growing?', "Who do you think you arc', 'Why are you seeking more?', all in the hope to demoralize you, dent your conviction, in the hope that you may give up in your pursuit and turn back and surrender to the old and familiar bondage of a Pharaoh, still of your own making.

As you decide and are determined to live out your calling, hold onto these promises, "Do not fear, for I am with you…", Isaiah 41:10, "…and lo, I am with you always, even to the end of the age." Matthew 2:20.

With this, you can now courageously step into the narrow path, for you are told not to fear, for Divine-Guidance is with you, infinite intelligence is with you, infinite supply – Almighty God is with you. Stop being someone you are not and doing work you know in your hearts of hearts you are not supposed to do. Step into the space you know is yours to occupy, the place you know is yours to fill – your unique self-expression – and shine your light unashamedly. Be courageous and move forward fearlessly, dare to trust the image of your vision, for in it sleeps the advice and the tools you need to make it real. Stretch your hand over your fear (this means keeping your minds-eye fixed right on your vision), and you will witness what you fear, the red sea dividing itself, (meaning all your obstacles disappearing), giving way to you, for nothing (and no obstacle) in the world can stop the power that is within you.

"For though we walk in the flesh, we do not war according to the flesh. For the weapons of our warfare *are* not carnal but mighty in God for pulling down strongholds, casting down arguments and every high thing that exalts itself against the knowledge of God, bringing every thought into captivity to" 2 Corinthians 10:3-5

So, fear not, if you find yourself in unfavorable circumstances and discouraging conditions. Like the mustard seed, re-root yourself by investing in your mind, for the mind is the greatest bank account you could ever deposit in. Acquire knowledge and new skills, study the blueprints of those who came and went before you, who are what you would like to be, who are doing what you would love to do, and who are having what you would love to have. Invest in yourself, dig for information, for even if the day comes, when everything in life closes down on you; They can take your money, your house away, your car, your spouse can abandon you, but one thing they will not and cannot take away from you is your knowledge. And providentially, you can use your acquired knowledge to rebuild your life from any start point.

So, you are to be patient in the meantime, enjoy the journey while moving in the direction of your dream, for God is building your character, preparing you for the big arena, of which you will be ready when the time has revealed itself. Most importantly, you will be well equipped to withstand the wildest weathers of adversity that might ever attempt to knock you down as you are endeavoring to attain your dream.

You are guaranteed to face hardships and challenges as you move towards the attainment of your desire, and the most pressing question that you are sure to be confronted with that, would demand a response is; are you going to behave like the sons of Israel? Will you be like those who, when it appeared as if they were trapped in the desert, were quick to judge by appearance and started bombarding Moses with questions? "Was it because there were no graves in Egypt that you brought us to the desert to die in the wilderness? Is this not the word that we spoke to you in Egypt, saying, 'Leave us alone that we may serve the Egyptians?' For it would have been better for us to serve the Egyptians than to die in the wilderness." Or are you going to listen to your intuition and look for the sign of the Lord in faith, even when all the doors of opportunity and advancement are seemingly being slammed in your face?

Now in this beautiful drama as recorded in scripture, the destination of Canaan represents your dream or the thing that you would love to be, do, or have. It is your dream that will bring you honey and milk, once attained. Moses means *faith and perseverance.* The sons of Israel represent *fear.* The *sea* portrays an obstacle. And Egypt means a *comfort zone* or *safe place.* Pharaoh represents bondage from your current energy-draining job or the unsatisfying life you are leading.

Once you are clear on your dream (Canaan), or what you would love to be, do, or have, you must now march on towards it. Be the Moses that you are, and fear not, wait on the sign from God as to what is the next best step or thing to do for you to maneuver through the *obstacle* you are faced with as you march towards your desire.

We are also told that *doubt and fear* will visit us along the way as we seek to advance towards our desire. In the world of the individual this may come in the form of ill opinions from friends or parents, fruitless advice from others as to why you cannot be, do, or have the thing that you would love, people laughing at your ideas, as men who don't the power of imagination often do, or business partners persuading you to abandon your ideas and let go of the business you dream of expanding and making it a success. Know these are the sons of Israel, or *fear*, quarrelling with you, condemning you, censuring as you attempt to free yourself from your current unsatisfying life and marching towards your dream.

Know that as you march towards your dream, you will face challenges and hardships along the way, and the voice of fear will bombard you, trying to convince you to turn back and go back to your comfort zone.

Do not entertain the voice of *fear*. Do not wish to go back to your place of safety, your comfort zone, to remain in bondage, a life you wish to walk away from, even if you are confronted with hardships along the way. Do not go back to the old and dreary, a job that makes you heavy and miserable, something that you do but against which your whole nature rebels, even if you think it provides comfort and security. Keep marching onward and upward, for in the right hour you will receive the sign to open the seemingly closed doors, and your fear and doubt will be left behind. The pharaoh of your old lifestyle will be buried in the deep sea behind you as you march heavenward.

The point intended in this drama is that we are never to pay attention to the voice of fear when we are faced with hardships and difficulties. We should in-turn turn to where our help cometh from, to the mountain, that far-away place within ourselves, the theater of our imagination, to ask what the next best action is that we are to take that would advance us in the direction of our dream. We must learn to wait on the voice of truth and of power for guidance – and to trust it. For if we but listen attentively, we are sure to be given the instructions that will allow us to march forward. Not around or in another direction, but through the face of the very thing that appears to be an obstacle to us, hindering us. It is made known to us, through this drama that the power and intelligence within us will make a way where there seems to be no way.

The 'how' – (the information and tools) needed to achieve any dream is never revealed at the beginning, it is dare I say a spiritual phenomenon, revealed and provided as one move along, and in truth, never ours to be concerned about. The way that our desires will come about is beyond our comprehension. It is contained within the realm of spirit - by your higher-self – the Greater one.

The truth of the above statement sleeps in the words of Jesus, "I and my father are One," and, "the Father is greater than I am."

Now you will be prompted to question what the words of Jesus have to do with you. Well, know that

Jesus also said, "I am in My Father, and you in Me, and I in you."

So, if we are in Jesus, and Jesus is in us, and in the Father, you can see why he said 'the Father is greater than I am,' for he too was trapped in the same garment of flesh and blood that we are trapped in. Thusly, the how, the instructions or the plans that will bring about our desire, will be provided to us by that which is greater than us - the Father. So, walk in faith, and trust the process, after all we are told, "...that He who began a good work in you will carry it on to completion..."

"Through Him (imagination) all things were made; without Him, nothing was made that has been made." So, it is to him we must turn if we wish to create the thing that we would love to create. For he also said,

"In My Father's house are many rooms. If it were not so, would I have told you that I am going there to prepare a place for you? And if I go and prepare a place for you, I will come back and welcome you into My presence, so that you also may be where I am."

"Lord," said Thomas, "we do not know where You are going, so how can we know the way?" And in answer to Thomas, we are being told how to create the thing we would love to create, for he said, "I am the way and the truth and the life." Who is the way, the truth and the life? Our own wonderful imagination.

Now the house that is referred to in this message by Jesus is not a terrestrial house and neither are the rooms, but in truth the philosophy gem of his message is that; in the world of thoughts (the Father's *house)*, are many *ideas* (the many *rooms*), and we must focus our attention and think of ourselves in such a way that matches the ideal life we wish to live, to visualizing our dream - meaning to go with our *imagination* to this place and prepare it, to live in the end to say. We can do this by impressing our desire or vision upon the womb of the Spirit, or by entering and dwelling through imagining, in its Spirit, and so mold the spiritual-prototype of our desire. This deliberately preparing a place in the future with our infinite-Spiritual-Self, a place that we are soon to enter and dwell in it, with our physical bodies, and be in the presence of the idea that we have *imagined*, (I will welcome you into My presence, so that you also may be where I am)."

Remember that it is the Life-Force or Spirit within us that gives life to things, and since the Spirit seeks to express itself through us, so in truth, the Spirit in us is the way, the truth and the life. Within us is a creative power that many a man has utilized unconsciously and thusly have designed their life by default, and if we can but become aware of it, we can harness and deliberately design and give life to any desire we would love to experience.

The information and ideas that will help us find our way towards the attainment of our desire are not at the frequency of our current situation, but at the frequency of our ideal. Mary Morrissey knows this truth because she wrote that, "If we can stabilize the frequency of our desired good in our feeling state as well as our mental state, we become much more attractive and time collapses." Years ago, Albert Einstein eloquently told us this same truth in his own unique way that, *"Everything is energy and that's all there is to it. Match the frequency of the reality you want and you cannot help but get that reality."*

We do not get what we want, but what we are. So, to get the thing we want, we must first become the energy of the thing we want. Aligning our thoughts, words and deeds with our desire will in turn allow us to become a vibrational match to the desire we seek. By consistently blending in the spirit and remaining with the feeling of the good we seek, we can thus attract the thing we want.

A gardener stretches his hand to sow a seed of corn in the earth, thus allowing the seed to rely and utilize the power within itself, to germinate, sprout and grow to be harvested. In this way, he can feed his home, his community or perhaps a nation at large. So, in the same way, we must stretch our imaginative hand and touch the fringe of the cloak of our desire, sowing the seed of the thing that we would love to be, do, or have in the soil of our mind. This allowing the desire to germinate, sprout and grow to be harvested.

This message is also hidden in the drama recorded in scripture about a woman who had been subject to bleeding for twelve years. Spending all her money on physicians had proven to be in vain. One day she came up behind Jesus, pushing herself amongst the people crowding around and pressing Jesus, and she touched the fringe of Jesus's cloak. Immediately her bleeding stopped. In this drama Jesus represents our *desire*, the crowd represents *obstacles,* and the woman represents *faith* and *focus*.

"Who touched me?" Jesus asked. "Someone touched Me, for I know that power has gone out from Me."

We must be like this woman, who dared to focus and walk in faith towards her desire. In like-manner, we must have the courage of our conviction and dare to navigate through the dire circumstances and other obstacles that might threaten to hinder us from attaining our desire and stretch out the hand of our imagination and in faith touch the fringe of our desire. Our desire, once realized by our touch, can heal and change our lives and the lives of our community and perhaps humanity at large.

"Until one is committed, there is hesitancy, the chance to draw back. Concerning all acts of initiative (and creation), there is one elementary truth, the ignorance of which kills countless ideas and splendid plans: that the moment one commits oneself, then Providence moves too. All sorts of things occur to help one that would never otherwise have occurred. A whole stream of events issues from the decision, raising in one's favor all manner of unforeseen incidents and meetings and material assistance, which no man could have dreamed would have come his way. Whatever you can do, or dream you can do, begin it. Boldness has genius, power, and magic in it. Begin it now." W.H. Murray.

Once you consciously decide to be the thing that you will, and do that which you will, and have that which you will, you will run into people who have information you will need, into circumstances that will point you in the right direction, and you will be guided to places that have resources that you can utilize. For if you but move, providence moves, too. Thus, never concern yourself about the 'how', for it will come – sure!

You don't have to know HOW,
the thing that you would love to be, do, or have will come
about; but still,
be the thing that you would love to be, and
do the things that you would love to do, and the
things you would love to have will be given unto you;
right WHERE you are

CHAPTER 5
WHERE?

Where and when to start

"Do not wait; the time will never be "just right". Start where you stand, and work with whatever tools you may have at your command, and better tools will be found as you go along." – Napoleon Hill

The question before every man is, *where* should I start in regards to pursuing my dreams or to be and do what I would love to?

We get what we are and what we believe, not what we want. So then, we must step up to what we would love to be, and start to do the things that we would love to do, and then we will be sure to earn the things that we would love to have, right where we are. Doing this, a man will align himself with and become a vibrational match to his desire. This allows the Law of Attraction to work in his favor without investing much thought or adhering to all the new age techniques of meditation and visualization that require such a great amount of discipline and effort. "As we are, so we do; and as we do, so is it done to us". So, we must become the source of what we seek, right where we are, and right in the now. This conduct will in turn allow us to attract the ideas, events, circumstances and people that will assist us to attain the thing we desire. This is the shortest and the most joyful creative route, and the only noble formula that would boost us into an arena of success and true abundance, and a place where excellence and freedom dwells.

I am a product of a country upbringing, raised by my grandmother in a reserve. Cattle, goats, sheep, and chickens were our dinner as well as our bank account. My grandmother was a very tidy woman, and her most pressing desire was to be in, and sleep in, a clean environment. She had all the means to feed and live luxuriously if she so wished to, but she was old-fashioned. Born in late 1922, she grew up during an era of oppression and apartheid in previously South West Africa, now named Namibia. She was a very conservative woman in her spending and conduct, as she was a product of humble beginnings. She would often remind me proudly during our late-night conversations. The only modern thing on her house was the corrugated iron roof-top and the floor that was made from concrete. The rest of the house was made of wood, cattle manure, and mud. She didn't have a broom like the rest of the family members in the compound, but her place was always tidy. When I grew up, I realized that she had made a broom from a cow's tail, and a feather duster from chicken feathers tied to a stick. Here was an uneducated woman who did not permit her environment to prevent her from achieving what she wanted. She wanted a clean and comfortable place to call home, and she got it. It gave her peace of mind and a sense of belonging, and she became resourceful to create tools from whatever she had at her disposal to achieve her desire.

The above story might not be of great significance; but the point to bring across is that of the ability to be resourceful. Wherever we are, with whatever we have, there are always things we can utilize that lie dormant. If noticed, they can easily be turned into tools that we can use to assist us in attaining the things we want. As one moves forward, progressing and growing, more tools will be available to him as he goes along.

Let me tell you another tale that will show you a glimpse of the truth stated in the foregoing statements. Consider the scripture that says, "Faith by itself, if it is not complemented by action, is dead."

When I was a boy in the country, the desire to visit big cities situated miles away would arise on many occasions, either for work, college, or simply for pleasure. Often, there would be no means of transport at home, but regardless, there lay within me a burning desire to make my way the big city. Since I had a reason as to why and for what I had to go, I refused to sit at home and bite my nails, waiting on God to bring me a ride from right where I was. I would take my little bag and go by the roadside to hitchhike. Sometimes I would wait there until sunset.

If nothing came by, I would go back home and sleep for the night, but I would be at the corner first thing in the morning, to wait until a ride came by. I would ask for a ride or pay a small fee to go to the nearest village, and I would continue to go in the direction of the big city. Sometimes, it took a day or two, or even up to three days to get to the big city, but still, I would make it. Sometimes, I would wait long enough without seeing any traffic that I was forced to go, by foot, to the next nearest village, hoping to get a ride to the next town until I made it to the big city. Many a times I would run into someone with reliable information that would find me a ride, which would then set me on the path to make it to the city. If we make but a little effort, little by little, persistently walking towards our desires, we are sure to arrive where we would love to be.

The English saying, "A journey of a thousand miles begins with a single step," addresses the above story. The Ovaherero ethnic group from Namibia have put it another way:(*Okunjonga njonga, okuyenda kumoi*) loosely translated; "One step at a time, is the way to your destination." The words of these profound phrases, however, are nothing alone, and they remain nothing but labels until they are employed. What matters is that they *are* employed and not merely uttered and taken for entertainment. So, the questions before you are; where are you headed? Are you taking the little, but necessary steps towards your vision? or the thing that you would love to be, do, or have? Or are you idling and waiting for a miracle from God that would transform your life? while

He has bestowed all the power and intelligence upon you?

Start where you are, and do what you can, with what you have, and better tools will be shown to you as you go along.

No matter where a man is placed in this world, he knows exactly what he would love to be, do, or have. Once filled with desire, he can always push himself to action, with whatever limited resources he has, to propel himself in the direction of becoming, doing, and having that which he would love to be, do, and have.

I know of a young man with a passion in soccer, who has shrugged off some hostile environments to now captain one of Namibia's prominent soccer teams, which he joined when he was but seventeen. I knew him, ages ago, as a boy in primary school, when I was but a boy as well. We all seemed confined to a pressing environment with limited resources. We would often play with soccer balls made from plastic bags covered with socks in the dusty playground of the school, and sometimes in the dusty streets of the village. I was soon to part from that school to pursue my further education elsewhere. While in college, I found myself having a conversation with someone who happened to come from the same village this young lad had come from. By now, he had blossomed into a well-known soccer star in the country. Although I had heard about him in the newspapers and through word of mouth, he was only ever mentioned through a nickname. Because of this, I had never realized it was him, as I could only remember his real name. During the conversation with this young lady, she happened to mention that very name. Instantly, it struck me with old memories flashing in the back of my mind. A proof of the universe creative principle I am conveying in this material was silently rendered to me in that very moment, of how this young boy had, perhaps, subconsciously made use of the creative principle of the universe to cut through all the challenges that he might have faced to achieve his dream of being a professional soccer player. He is proof sufficient that there is no more precious action in the world than inspired action, and to do something that you are passionate about is the most important victory you can achieve. In recent years, Oprah Winfrey put this truth in simple yet profound terms when she said, "The biggest adventure you can ever take is to live the life of your dreams."

There are always opportunities silently waiting to be noticed and utilized, but one must know what he would love to be, do, or have for him to be able to notice the opportunities and the information, that would propel him in the direction of his desire.

Wherever you are on your journey towards your desire, you must hold tightly onto your desire and keep feeding your mind with your vision in order to develop the much-needed faith, for in scripture we are told that, "faith comes from what is heard". Faith will in turn propel you to action, and action will lead you to the plans and ideas that were seemingly invisible. Once visible, you can utilize these ideas meaningfully to propel you in the direction of your heart's desire.

Even if your desire cannot be easily catered by your current environment, which may be lacking in opportunities to grant you advancement and growth; No matter how discouraging your present outlook, hold onto your vision nevertheless. In due time, the universe will tweak and reposition things in your favor to advance you to an environment that will assist you in manifesting your dream. Infinite intelligence penetrates and permeates all space, and your Higher-Self, or Who You Really Are, is an integral component of the very Spirit which occupies all space. Because of this, nothing is impossible.

The adage, "bloom where you are planted," has a greater significance than the skeletal meaning generally attached to it. The word '*bloom*' calls you forth to begin to sprout, calling you to action, to rise and seek the light that would assist you, so that you may bear fruit and thereby express the beauty and the greatness within you.

Bloom in the now, right where you are, where life has you balanced this point in time. "Do not wait for a change of environment, before you act; get a change of environment by action." A better environment will come on its own, at the right time, and when you are fully prepared for it. This change of environment will present itself in line with your readiness, willingness, and persistence as you keep on moving towards the attainment of the thing that you would love to be, do, or have.

The last word in the adage is "planted." Regardless of how you got where you are, whether you believe that circumstances are predetermined or that some external forces beyond your control placed you where you are, the message remains, "*Bloom where you are planted.*" We create our own reality, no matter where we are. So, by comprehending and becoming aware of this truth, one can start creating his own reality deliberately by design and not by default right where he is. It is because of the eternal gifts of free will and choice, gifts that no man could ever take away from you, that you can begin at once to bloom right where you are, with what you have. If you do that, the road ahead will unfold itself. The next step to be taken will reveal itself, if you but exhaust the one step in front of you that you can take.

"'Let there be,' God said, and there was." Where? Right where he was, out of consciousness, and out of the womb and essence of Spirit. "Allow," He said. He did not have the means outside of Him, but He had all the means within Him. There was no external form available from which he created the light. He did not wait for a change of circumstances, or a change of environment, or change of finances. Not from outwards, but from within he called the light into being. We are told that we were created in His image and 'likeness', which means we too have within us the ability to call forth our desires out of seemingly dark circumstances, out of seemingly void environments, and out of seemingly empty bank accounts and bring them into being.

Wherever you are planted, God has only noble plans for you. He has "plans for welfare and not for calamity, plans to give you a future and a hope."

There is a common principle in every religion known to men. It is a principle of 'faith.' Every master that walks and has ever walked the face of the earth has told and continues to instruct us to not judge only by appearance.

There is hope where you are, and there are opportunities where you are. Once you realize that there is greatness within you seeking to express itself through your body, you will then realize that the prison gates that you thought had slammed behind you, are actually ajar. You can walk to the gates and open them by asking a simple question every day. "What can I do today with what I have and where I am, that can move me towards the thing that I would love to be, do, and have?"

There is nothing in this terrestrial world that exists entirely on its own and without contrast. Where good is, evil resides, and vice-versa. Any environment and any circumstance bears within its arrangement both the elements of opportunity and of misfortune. Napolean Hill said, "Every adversity brings with it the seed of an equivalent advantage." If that statement is true without variation, then every unfavorable environment must also bring with it the seed of equal advantage, and every dire circumstance must also bring with it the seed of favorable one.

The Ovaherero ancestors also knew this truth very well when they said, "There is no home ever-so lovely and perfect, that the bad cannot creep in." But they, knowing this truth, should have told us to also flip the coin on this ancient adage and realize that it also means, "There is no home so troubled that there is no room for good to creep in." They should have told us that, there is no circumstance or an environment so hostile that it has no room for some good that we can notice and utilize to advance us in the direction of our dreams. They should have told us that, in the bad also sleeps the seed of good.

Wherever you are, the prison walls around you are of your own making and, so are the gates ajar. The prison gates have only been slammed in your mind and through your own thinking. And because they have been closed in your mind, you can walk right up to the gates and swing them open with your revived imagination coupled with your brand-new way of thinking, thinking the right-way, thinking along the lines of truth, along the lines of life, thinking noble thoughts and thoughts of good report. Once you practice this truth, free you will be set, first within and then without, for as it is in heaven so shall it be on earth, right where you are, as your environment will begin to mirror back to you, the manifested physical equivalents of your revived inner-most thoughts.

Until someone came along and harnessed it, by developing an apparatus with rotating blades that creates a current of air for cooling and for ventilation, air however, was ever present but no man thought of the idea to harness and utilized it in this fashion. Likewise, was the means of producing electricity - ever been present, unrealized however, until someone came along and constructed them into a system that would generate electrical power. The Intelligence from which we have come from, is right where we are, and lies ever dormant in the absence of our awareness and realization of its presence. We can find this truth in "I will never leave you nor forsake you", and also, "I stand at the door and knock". This Being that will never abandon you and standing at your door and knocking is not a Being outside of you. It is the very Intelligence that molded you into being. It is the current of life itself that penetrates, permeates, and fills all space. And just like the air and electricity, it is always readily available to be harnessed and allowed to express itself through whatsoever the medium the individual wills. The only thing required is for us to recognize and become aware of it, of its presence and availability. And as a man would build an incandescent bulb through which electricity would express itself, so should he create a mode around the lines of his own unique pattern of self-expression through which the Spirit within him can begin to flow and express itself. Right where you are, the Intelligence of life that fuels and resurrects dreams and gives them form - is present.

Henry David Thoreau prompts us to march onward by giving us a glimpse of what could happen in the future, He gives us an idea of the unknown we so often fear, thus remaining in our comfort zones. He gives us a partial view of the good possibilities and opportunities that lies in the road ahead, in the hope that we may develop the courage to start advancing in the direction of our dreams, this is what he had in mind we he uttered, "If one advances confidently in the direction of his dreams, and endeavors to live the life which he has imagined, he will meet with a success unexpected in common hours. He will put some things behind, will pass an invisible boundary; new, universal, and more liberal laws will begin to establish themselves around and within him; or the old laws be expanded, and interpreted in his favor in a more liberal sense, and he will live with the license of a higher order of beings."

For a man to advance in the direction of his dreams, he has to know with definite purpose what he would love to be, do, or have, and begin at once to imagine, feel, inhabit, and incarnate his vision right where he is.

Be what you would love to be,
right WHERE you are and,
start doing the things you would love to do,
right WHERE you are and,
the things you would love to have will be given unto you;
you don't have to know WHEN.

– Muzire Mbuende (2016)

CHAPTER 6
WHEN?

When your dream will actualize

"If you wait until all the lights are "green" before you leave home, you'll never get started on your trip to the top." - Zig Ziglar

In the pursuit of his vision, every man asks himself, 'When will my dream come true?'

The manifestation of a dream does not know and neither does it depend on time as man has come to understand time. In life, there is only a time to sow, a time for germination (a period where the caused undergoes a biological process in order to develop fully and), and a time to harvest. There is a time for the mind to conceive an idea, a period for the mind to clothe the idea, and a time to give birth to the idea in its physical equivalent into the visible world. Scripture tells us that, "with all things for which you pray and ask, believe that you have received them, and they will be granted to you." So, turn to the daily affairs of your life in faith, and trust that whatever you have prayed for has already been granted unto you, and will show itself in due time.

Every idea we will ever conceive already exists. Everything we will ever desire already exists, either in physical form or as a formless spiritual prototype and a mere possibility. And the moment we focus on an idea long enough, the circumstances and channels that will lead us to the attainment of this idea also begin to establish themselves instantaneously. This is what is meant with, "…While they are still talking about their needs, I will go ahead and answer their prayers." However, what is required from us in return is the effort and discipline of impressing our desire consistently with cutting edge clarity into the soil of our mind. This is required in order to give specification and total assurance to our mind that we undoubtedly want it to grow the seed that we have buried in its womb, and not leave the mind to treat our desire as a mere thought floating by. It is only through repeated suggestion that assurance is given to the mind. Once that assurance is given, the seemingly invisible, yet already established circumstances and events will soon begin to come into our view to be seized.

This is the promise of God. There is no rule of thumb as to when exactly in our worldly time God will grant our hearts desires. His promise is this; the moment you conceive a desire, it is given! The vision of your dream is not a mere figment of the imagination, but a spiritual prototype of your dream and ideal life shown to you by

God, and a confirmation that the thing that you have ask, has been granted to you. It is an assurance of the thing hoped for. Then, through focusing on our desire and assuring the mind of what we want it to clothe, it remains only a matter of time for the already established channels to begin to come into view. Then your job becomes clear. It will be required of you to partake in doing the task that is required as furnished by every opportunity, thus moving you in the direction of your dream. It is through faith and a burning desire that we hold steadfast the unseen prototype of our desire in our minds eye. But, it is through constant action and intelligent effort that we are sure to walk towards our desire and to obtaining it. We must keep in mind that the body as a vehicle of spirit must do what it was created to do. The body is not created to remain idle. It has a role to play, together with the mind and spirit to help create and make our desires actualize, and that is to move, so it must move.

It is unnecessary to write about the times and the seasons, for your desire is sure to come, but it will come to you like a thief at night. Therefore, keep watch, because we do not know the day when the thing that we would love to be, do, or have will come. For this reason, you also must be ready, because your desire, will come at an hour when you least expect it.

Keep watch of the circumstances and opportunities that will show themselves as signals and aid, with the intention to prompt you to the works you must do, in order to propel you in the direction of your desires.

"Ask, and it will be given to you; seek, and you will find; knock, and it will be opened to you."

This is the promise. Any other advice and instructions you may receive that are not akin to this truth should be disregarded. When they say lo here or lo there, follow them not. Be intolerant of the beliefs you think are to set you in the wrong direction. Cling solely to the truth that you have come to know; that although you cannot see your desire - it is given, and it is sure to actualize in the material plane.

"Ask and it will be given to you," are the words of the Christ. He never said, "Ask if you are highly educated, or if you have a college degree, or if you are from a certain background, or if you belong to this or that ethnic group". His words leave us not in ambiguity, for he put it simply and in so clear a language that, a child can understand: 'Ask and it will be given to you'. That is the promise and the secret of manifestation. Cling onto to that promise and the power and the truth of these words will soon begin to reveal themselves in your own experience.

He is a powerful God, but he is sure not a bulldozer. The God of Abraham, Isaac and Jacob is not a God of muscle and favoritism. He will not elbow any man out of the way in order to grant you your desire. Neither will He deliver your desire unto you on the backs of small men. Everything He ever did, does, and will ever do is for the highest good of all, and for the benefit of all involved. Every man, woman, or child involved in the transaction of delivering your desire will receives the thing that they would love to have and are sent about their way in peace and harmony. If it takes two men to play a role in granting you your desire, or the thing that you would love to have, so will it be. If it takes a hundred men, the process will unfold accordingly. If it will take five thousand men to bring your desire about, men will queue accordingly and will play their role to the hilt, and every man in the queue will be granted what they seek in return. For the ways of God are harmonious and non-turbulent. Look to the words of the Lord to Zerubbabel, where He said, "'Not by might nor by power, but by My Spirit,' says the lord of hosts." Not by muscle, but through His Spirit that penetrates, permeates and fills all space of the universe and evermore.

Once you have asked, seek to become what you would love to be, and do what you can do, where you are, with what you have. Constantly do the deeds, however small, that are in alignment with your desire. It is not the magnitude of your being-ness or of your doing-ness that is significant, but the attitude. This will align you with the creative powers of the universe, and by law a sevenfold akin to your attitude will be given back you. Do not ask as to when it is going to come, for in the same fashion as his ways are past finding out, so is his hour also, past finding out. Simply clothe yourself with the promise given unto you and soon, in an hour you can never know, your desire will be externalized.

"God is not human, that he should lie, not a human being, that he should change his mind. Does he speak and then not act? Does he promise and not fulfill?" That is the promise of the indescribable One who feels all space. What power and authority are in these words!

Just as a Gardener nurtures the seed of corn he has sowed in the dark womb of the earth with water and nutrients, and by keeping it free from weeds, so should you nurture your desire by organizing and disciplining your thoughts and actions to be in alignment with your ideal and by flick away the thoughts of fear that would attempt to suffocate your desire. Ensure your desire is well nurtured, by investing in yourself and upgrading your knowledge and skills, through programs and material that are in alignment with your desire. Remain faithful that sooner or later the sprout of the desire that you have sown in the soil of your mind will soon push through, seeking the light to bear fruit that would benefit you and humanity at large.

As a gardener would go about his daily affairs in faith after sowing his seed and not engage in secret prayers, rituals, and begging for the seed to germinate, or to sprout, or to grow, and to bear fruit, so should you remain faithful that your desire will externalized itself in a timely manner. In a like manner, as you could care less as to the biological process, or *how* the seed undergoes its process of seeking the light, so should you care less as to *how* the spiritual process of the invisible unfolds itself to bring about your desire. All we ever want is to eventually harvest the desire that we have sown, but patience and virtue must come first.

We must be constantly disciplined in order to direct our focus and deeds towards the thing that we would love to be, do, or have, in the same way as we would put bits into the mouths of horses to guide them towards the destination we have set for ourselves. Just as a Landlord would guard his property, keeping it free from bad tenants and keeping the ones that are loyal and obedient, so should a man guard the property of his mind, guarding against impure and useless thoughts of fear that try to overwhelm him. This way he can then keep moving towards his own success and his freedom with only the tenants of lovely and of a behavior of good report. By pursuing this process, a man is soon to discover that he is the Landlord of his mind. He is also soon to find himself in an arena of grace and beauty where freedom and influence dwells. As Landlords of our own minds we should rid of bad thoughts from entering the property of our minds, for not only will they affect us financially, but also spiritually, emotionally, and consequently our physical bodies will begin to suffer eventually.

Your dream will come to pass, but only in a time that the womb of creation has set for it. Known to itself. The words of Neville Goddard come to mind, and I am going to paraphrase here as I do not have his exact terms in front of me. But he said something along the lines of, "Your dream will come true, and it can be within three weeks like it takes a chicken egg to hatch. It might be after one full month just like a rabbit. It could happen after nine months like it takes a human being to give birth. Or eleven months like a horse." Or perhaps you will have to wait for twenty years like it take an oak to bear an acorn! Therefore, just plant your seed firmly in the womb of creation, keep on clothing it with faith, and go about your way. It will undoubtedly come to pass. It is law - sure.

Worry not, for you can never know the timing of the womb of creation. Be obstinate in seeking your dream, "For yet in a very little while, He who is coming will come, and will not delay." Walk in faith and keep on knocking. Keep knocking, not once or twice, but a thousand times, for those who come to test the door knob once or twice will be proven unsuccessful. Knock persistently, and the thing that you would love to have will be given to you.

We are told a great story in scripture by the Nazarene, that, suppose one of your friends has come to you on a journey, and you have nothing to set before him, so you go to your neighboring friend at midnight and ask him to lend you three loaves of bread, so you can set before your visiting friend. And the friend answers from the inside, "Do not bother me. My door is already shut and my children are with me in bed. I cannot get up to give you anything." In this great parable, we are told if we persist in knocking, kindly but with passion, it will be solely because of our persistence that our friend will have no choice but to get up and give us much more than we need. This story has been fulfilled by a great number of successful individual in the visible world.

Early in her career pursuit, Oprah Winfrey was fired from her job as a reporter because she was told she was unfit for TV. Because she knew what she wanted to be and do, she was persistent and went on to become the host of her own program, "The Oprah Winfrey Show," and later launching her own TV Network, the Oprah Winfrey Network or "OWN". Today, this inspiring woman is well known around the globe, even in the unknown and the forgotten parts of the world.

Cut from his high school basketball team for a "lack of skill," a young Michael Jordan went home, locked himself in the privacy of his bedroom, and cried. But because he knew what he wanted to be and do in life, he was persistent and continued to play the game he loved, and later became the greatest basketball player the world of basketball has seen of his generation.

Let us also center our attention to the fact that these brilliant individuals were not seeking things or wanting to accumulate the accessories of life as the average man has come to understand life when they started pursuing their dreams. They simply employed the paradigm; BE, DO, and then HAVE, which is the principle intended and conveyed throughout this material. They worked with the creative power of the universe and hence, were rewarded abundantly. For we are told to first seek the kingdom of God and the rest shall be added unto us. Seek your calling, your vision, your life's work and the accessories of life will be added unto you. That is the secret to a joyful and successful life.

So, we must decline discouragement due to the opinion of our fellow men and persist in seeking the thing that we would love to be, do, or have. For just as the friend in scripture, the man who has the thing that you are seeking will have no choice but to get up and give it to you if we but persist in our endeavor. Keep on seeking, for you will find what you would be, do, and have. Keep on knocking, for concealed opportunity will awaken when you show you will not give up.

Be what you would love to be,
right in this moment and,
do the things you would love to do,
right in this moment and,
the things you would love to have will be given unto you;
you don't have to know WHEN; but it is already given.

– Muzire Mbuende (2016)

Chapter 7
Summary

Your physical body is God's medium, through which He seeks to express and experience Him-self. The Spirit or the Father in you (**Who** You Really Are) seeks to be harnessed and be guided by you to be able to fully express Itself in a distinct manner along the lines of your own unique self-expression. Thus, you must know exactly **what** you would love to be and do, for there is a vision planted in the inside of you, seeking to express, explore and experience itself. You have a noble purpose, a divine mission to fulfil on earth - for this you are, for this you exist – sure.

It is imperative to know **why** you would love to be and do that which you would love to be and do, for your *'why'* is the fuel that will carry you through tough and challenging times. Your motive must be noble and of good report. Mainly to serve others and for the betterment and advancement of life Itself. It should not be a motive of acquiring money or the accessories of life. To seek to acquire things in life is to start on a wrong footing. It is a method that will cause you to work against the creative powers of the universe. Your reason behind wanting to be that which you would love to be must be greater than your excuses, lack of skills, or lack of education. With this attitude, you will do everything in your power achieve your dream, and eventually your excuses and reasons will pack their bags and leave, for they cannot reside where courage, determination and faith dwells.

Do not concern yourself with *how* your dream will actualize. It is a process that is beyond human understanding. The means and plans of your desire lies within the desire itself. The tools and information you will need and the direction you must take at any point in time will be presented and shown to you in a timely manner as you move along. In the meantime, keep doing what you can, with what you have, right where you are.

Start immediately, right *where* you are, and the resources and information that once and seemingly laid dormant will become clear to you, and you can utilize them to propel you in the direction of your dreams. Walk with the end goal in mind. Having the destination in mind yields the plans and the means to get you at your destination.

Do not be concerned as to *when* your desire will come to pass. As much as God's ways are past finding out, so is his timing. Find comfort, peace, and patience in the truth that once you have asked for the thing that you wish to be, it is given. Begin at once to be what you would love to be, and start doing what you would love to do, going about your daily affairs, and before you know it, at a time you least expect, that which you desire will be externalized.

FINAL WORD

I would like to finish this book with a quote from Les Brown:

"If you want a thing bad enough to go out and fight for it,
to work day and night for it, to give up your time, your peace
and your sleep for it…
If all that you dream and scheme is about it,
and life seems useless and worthless without it…
And if you gladly sweat for it and fret for it and plan for it and
lose all your terror of the opposition for it…
And if you simply go after that thing that you want with all of
your capacity, strength and sagacity, faith, hope and confidence
and stern pertinacity…
If neither cold, poverty, famish, nor gout, sickness nor pain, of
body and brain, can keep you away from the thing that you
want…
If dogged and grim you beseech and beset it,
with the help of God, you will get it!"
– Les Brown

THE END

REFERENCES

1. Walsch, D, N, N.(1998) *Conversation With God* Book Three. **angels-heaven.org**, **cosmic-people.com**

2. Tzu, L. Available from: **http://www.goodreads.com/quotes/645596 4-at-the-center-of-your-being-you-have-the-answer**

3. John 11:25. *New American Standard Bible*, US, National Publishing Company.

4. Deuteronomy 30:19. *New American Standard Bible*, US, National Publishing Company.

5. Proverbs 4:7. *New American Standard Bible*, US, National Publishing Company.

6. John 14:16. *New American Standard*

7. 1 John 4:4. *New American Standard Bible*, US, National Publishing Company.

8. *Bible*, US, National Publishing Company.

9. John 15:5-6. *New American Standard Bible*, US, National Publishing Company.

10. 1 Corinthians 2:11. *New American Standard Bible*, US, National Publishing Company.

11. John 15:8. *New American Standard Bible*, US, National Publishing Company.

12. Einstein, A. (2011). Available from: (**http://hillaryrubin.com/what-is-happiness/**)

13. Mann, H. (2014). Available from: **http://consciouslifenews.com/living-dream-les-brown/1174995/#**

14. Marden, S, O.(1917) *How To Get What You Want.* Timeless Wisdom Collection, Business and Leadership Publishing.

15. Hebrews 13:5. *New American Standard Bible*, US, National Publishing Company.

16. Proverbs 29:18. *New American Standard Bible*, US, National Publishing Company.

17. Revelation 3:20. *New American Standard Bible*, US, National Publishing Company.

18. Picasso, P. Available from: **http://www.goodreads.com/quotes/607827-the-meaning-of-life-is-to-find-your-gift-the**

19. 1 John 4:4. *New American Standard Bible*, US, National Publishing Company.

20. Matthew 11:27. *New American Standard Bible*, US, National Publishing Company.

21. Nichols, L. (2016). *Motivating The Masses.* Available from: **https://www.youtube.com/watch?v=D6X5c QjEOZI**

22. Psalm 133:1-3. *New American Standard Bible*, US, National Publishing Company.

23. Einstein, A. Available from: **http://www.values.com/inspirational-quotes/6131-everybody-is-a-genius-but-if-you-judge-a-fish**

24. John 15:2. *New American Standard Bible*, US, National Publishing Company.

25. Mathew 6:33. *New American Standard Bible*, US, National Publishing Company.

26. John 1:3. *New American Standard Bible*, US, National Publishing Company.

27. Mathew 6:9. *New American Standard Bible*, US, National Publishing Company.

28. Luke 17:21. *New American Standard Bible*, US, National Publishing Company.

29. Matthew 5:16. *New American Standard Bible*, US, National Publishing Company.

30. Brown, L. Available from: **http://www.goodreads.com/quotes/884712-the-graveyard-is-the-richest-place-on-earth-because-it**

31. Psalm 27:8. *New American Standard Bible*, US, National Publishing Company.

32. Psalm 23. *New American Standard Bible*, US, National Publishing Company.

33. Patanjali. Available from: **http://www.goodreads.com/quotes/337352-**

when-you-are-inspired-by-some-great-purpose-some-extraordinary

34. Matthew 14:22-31. *New American Standard Bible*, US, National Publishing Company.

35. 1 Corinthians 2:9. *New American Standard Bible*, US, National Publishing Company.

36. Einstein, A. (2015). Available from: **http://abridgetoyou.com.au/2015/01/if-you-want-to-lead-a-happy-life-tie-it-to-a-goal-not-to-people-or-things-albert-einstein/**

37. Luke 12:31. *New American Standard Bible*, US, National Publishing Company.

38. Proverbs 18:16. *New American Standard Bible*, US, National Publishing Company.

39. Galatian 6:7. *New American Standard Bible*, US, National Publishing Company.

40. John 1:1. *New American Standard Bible*, US, National Publishing Company.

41. John 1:14. *New American Standard Bible*, US, National Publishing Company.

42. di,M.Availablefrom: **https://www.brainyquote.com/quotes/quotes/m/mahatmagan109075.html**

43. John 1:1. *New American Standard Bible*, US, National Publishing Company.

44. John 1:14. *New American Standard Bible*, US, National Publishing Company.

45. Allen, J. As a Man Thinketh. Available from: **https://wahiduddin.net/thinketh/as_a_ma n_thinketh.pdf**

46. Genesis 1:3. *New American Standard Bible*, US, National Publishing Company.

47. Zechariah 4:6. *New American Standard Bible*, US, National Publishing Company.

48. Job 11. *New American Standard Bible*, US, National Publishing Company.

49. Luke 1:34. *New American Standard Bible*, US, National Publishing Company.

50. Tennyson, A. Available from: **http://izquotes.com/quote/315699**

51. Luke1:37-38,45. *New American Standard Bible*, US, National Publishing Company.

52. Morrissey, MM. Available from: **http://www.marymorrissey.com**. Life Mastery Institute.

53. James 2:17. *New American Standard Bible*, US, National Publishing Company.

54. Hebrew 11:1. *New American Standard Bible*, US, National Publishing Company.

55. Sagan, C. Available form: **https://www.brainyquote.com/quotes/quot es/c/carlsagan589698.html**

56. Acts 17:28. *New American Standard Bible*, US, National Publishing Company.

57. Zechariah 4:6. *New American Standard Bible*, US, National Publishing Company.

58. Luke 17:6. *New American Standard Bible*, US, National Publishing Company.

59. Exodus 14:11-12. *New American Standard Bible*, US, National Publishing Company.

60. Hill, N. (1937), *Think and Grow Rich.* Napoleon Hill Foundation, The Ralston Society.

61. John 10:30. *New American Standard Bible*, US, National Publishing Company.

62. John 14:28. *New American Standard Bible*, US, National Publishing Company.

63. John 14:20. *New American Standard Bible*, US, National Publishing Company.

64. John 1:3. *New American Standard Bible*, US, National Publishing Company.

65. John 14:2-3. *New American Standard Bible*, US, National Publishing Company.

66. John 14:1-6. *New American Standard Bible*, US, National Publishing Company.

67. Morrissey, MM. Available from: **http://www.marymorrissey.com**. Life Mastery Institute.

68. Einstein, A. Available from: **http://quoteinvestigator.com/2012/05/16/ev erything-energy/**

69. Luke 8:43-45. *New American Standard Bible*, US, National Publishing Company.

70. Murray, W, H. Available from: **http://www.goodreads.com/quotes/67769-until-one-is-committed-there-is-hesitancy-the-chance-to-Company**.

71. Hill, N. (1937), *Think and Grow Rich.* Napoleon Hill Foundation, The Ralston Society.

72. Emerson, W, R. Available from: **http://www.goodreads.com/quotes/548362-as-we-are-so-we-do-and-as-we-do**

73. James 2:17. *New American Standard Bible*, US, National Publishing Company.

74. Winfrey, O. Available from: **http://www.goodreads.com/quotes/8798-the-biggest-adventure-you-can-ever-take-is-to-live**

75. Roman 10:17. *New American Standard Bible*, US, National Publishing Company.

76. Wattles, W. *The Science of Getting Rich.* Greater Minds Ltd, **GreaterMinds.com**

77. Genesis 1:3. *New American Standard Bible*, US, National Publishing Company.

78. John 1:2. *New American Standard Bible*, US, National Publishing Company.

79. John 1:1. *New American Standard Bible*, US, National Publishing Company.

80. Matthew 6:25. *New American Standard Bible*, US, National Publishing Company.

81. Matthew 13-14. *New American Standard Bible*, US, National Publishing Company.

82. Matthew 6:33. *New American Standard Bible*, US, National Publishing Company.

83. Matthew 7:7. *New American Standard Bible*, US, National Publishing Company.

84. (Joel 3:10). *New American Standard Bible*, US, National Publishing Company.

85. Jeremiah 29:11. *New American Standard Bible*, US, National Publishing Company.

86. Hill, N. (1937), *Think and Grow Rich.* Napoleon Hill Foundation, The Ralston Society.

87. Deuteronomy 31:6. *New American Standard Bible*, US, National Publishing Company.

88. Revelation 3:20. *New American Standard Bible*, US, National Publishing Company.

89. Thoreau, D, H. Available from: **https://www.brainyquote.com/quotes/quot es/h/henrydavid163655.html**

90. Ziglar, Z. (2013). Available from: **https://www.facebook.com/ZigZiglar/post s/10151376508537863**

91. Mark 11:24. *New American Standard Bible*, US, National Publishing Company.

92. Isaiah 65:24. *New American Standard Bible*, US, National Publishing Company.

93. Mathew 7:7. *New American Standard Bible*, US, National Publishing Company.

94. Zechariah 4:6. *New American Standard Bible*, US, National Publishing Company.

95. Numbers 23:19. *New American Standard Bible*, US, National Publishing Company.

96. James 2:17. *New American Standard Bible*, US, National Publishing Company.

97. Hebrew 11:1. *New American Standard Bible*, US, National Publishing Company.

98. Hebrew 10:37. *New American Standard Bible*, US, National Publishing Company.

99. Luke 11:15. *New American Standard Bible*, US, National Publishing Company.

100. Brown, l. (2015). Available from: **http://www.bekerv.com/2015/07/if-you-want-a-thing-bad-enough/**

46035760R00097

Made in the USA
Lexington, KY
22 July 2019